How a Region Grows

Area Development in the U. S. Economy

By Harvey S. Perloff

with Vera W. Dodds

March, 1963

Based on *Regions, Resources and Economic Growth*
by Harvey S. Perloff, Edgar S. Dunn, Jr.,
Eric E. Lampard, and Richard F. Muth,
a study prepared for Resources For The Future, Inc.

GREENWOOD PRESS, PUBLISHERS
WESTPORT, CONNECTICUT

Library of Congress Cataloging in Publication Data

Perloff, Harvey S.
How a region grows.

Reprint. Originally published: New York : Committee for Economic Development, 1963.
1. United States--Economic conditions--Regional disparities. 2. Regional economics. I. Dodds, Vera W. II. Title.
HC103.P43 1984 338.973 84-691
ISBN 0-313-23152-4 (lib. bdg.)

Reprinted in 1984 by Greenwood Press
A division of Congressional Information Service, Inc.
88 Post Road West, Westport, Connecticut 06881

Printed in the United States of America

10 9 8 7 6 5 4 3 2 1

Contents

TABLES

FIGURES

AREA DEVELOPMENT ADVISORY BOARD

Foreword

HOW A REGION GROWS, *Area Development in the U. S. Economy,* by Harvey S. Perloff with the assistance of Vera W. Dodds, is the fifth Supplementary Paper to be published by the Area Development Committee of CED and the seventeenth in the CED series. It will provide businessmen, civic leaders and market researchers with a summary of the major forces affecting the location of employment within the United States. It is published in the belief that it will contribute to an understanding of some of the broad regional and national forces which influence growth or decline in each state and community.

The volume is based on a major research project undertaken by Resources For The Future and published under the title *Regions, Resources, and Economic Growth* (1960). The length of that volume (over 700 pages) and its mass of detail were obstacles to its use by many people who have a practical interest in regional economic development.

This Supplementary Paper compresses the major points of the large volume and expresses them in less technical language. In addition, it includes more recent data from the 1958 Census of Manufactures and the 1960 Census of Population. Edgar S. Dunn, Jr. has contributed some analysis of the more recent data for this volume. Sources for all the tables and figures are brought together in an Appendix at the end of the book. Scholars who have not worked through the earlier volume may find the present one an excellent introduction to the subject.

How a Region Grows starts with an historical description of the economic development of the various regions within the United States from 1870 together with an analytical discussion of the broad factors affecting the location of economic activity. It then proceeds to a detailed statistical analysis of the state-by-state movement of employment between the 1939 Census of Manufactures and 1958. Total employment is broken down into major industrial groups and the movement of each is examined.

Three industries – mining, agriculture, and manufacturing – stand out as having contributed most heavily to shifts in employment in the past two decades. Accordingly, three separate chapters discuss the internal changes within these industries and the geographic shifts in location which have resulted. Many of the reasons for the development of key industries in the various major regions of the country and in the individual states are explained.

The record of the shift in industrial location and its impact on different local markets will help in trying to estimate future trends for industries or areas. While this study deals primarily with broad regions and entire states, the same principles and trends often can be applied to single metropolitan areas. The present volume helps to put the economy of a state and community into a broad regional and national perspective.

The shifts in employment over the past two decades have brought to some areas boom conditions which have driven up local price levels. At the same time, other areas have experienced prolonged depression, even during periods of national prosperity. The latter problem and suggestions for dealing with it were discussed by the CED Research and Policy Committee in a Statement on National Policy, *Distressed Areas in a Growing Economy* (1961). In his concluding chapters Perloff expands on this problem and suggests some ways to facilitate adjustment. One chapter is devoted specifically to state and regional changes in per capita income and the usefulness of this measure of economic well being. The author points out that out-migration from areas of low employment often leads to a higher per capita income for those who remain.

The last chapter is devoted to programs which may help bring a better balance of labor force and employment opportunity. The suggestions are relevant both to areas of prolonged high unemployment and to areas which are uncertain about their prospects for future growth.

Uneven growth rates are to some extent inevitable in an economy as large and varied as that of the United States. However, they can create local inflation in some areas, putting upward pressure on the national average price level, and prolonged depression in other areas, contributing to a high level of national unemployment. Better understanding of the forces producing these geographic shifts in employment opportunities may help to lessen both local inflationary and local depressing forces, and in this way contribute to greater stability and growth for the nation.

John H. Nixon
Director of Area Development

Introduction

Basically this book is a condensed version of an earlier work published in 1960 by The Johns Hopkins Press for Resources for the Future, Inc. under the title *Regions, Resources, and Economic Growth*. The present volume, however, employs more recent statistical data and contains new material intended to clarify the data's implications in terms of general concepts of regional economic development and policy considerations.

The earlier book presented the results of a collaborative study carried out within the program of regional studies at Resources for the Future by three university scholars – Edgar S. Dunn, Jr., of the University of Florida, Eric E. Lampard, of the University of Wisconsin, and Richard F. Muth, of the University of Chicago – and myself. While its main purpose was to deepen understanding of the forces behind different rates of regional growth and to provide an improved conceptual and methodological framework for research in resources and regions, it also tried to provide information useful to public and private groups concerned with various aspects of economic growth.

Because the book was large (714 pages with 225 tables and 96 charts) and essentially technical in nature – we found the subject to be like a deep mine yielding its product only to probing with elaborate machinery – the question arose as to whether it was an appropriate means for communicating with busy persons whose responsibilities are for policy and action. We were strongly encouraged by groups interested in the field to produce a smaller and less technical version. The officers of the Committee for Economic Development, with whom we had been in close contact throughout all phases of our work, suggested that they would like to include a briefer version of the study in their Area Development series of research monographs. This book was prepared in response to that suggestion.

Collaboration with the CED has always been rewarding for us – and this book is no exception. I am grateful to Alfred C. Neal, President of CED, and John Nixon, Director of Area Development, for their encouragement and guidance in this undertaking. Mr. Nixon made a thorough review of the manuscript and played a large part in improving it.

I owe a very heavy debt to Messrs. Dunn, Lampard, and Muth, for, while this version was freshly written and introduces new material, in a very real sense they share in the authorship of this book as well as of the parent study. I owe an additional debt to Edgar S. Dunn, Jr., for his preparation of certain of the raw data on interstate industry "shifts" between 1939 and 1958. I wish also to acknowledge the contributions to the data and thinking by Otis Dudley Duncan and my colleague Lowdon Wingo, Jr. that have gone into this volume; I have drawn on materials which were prepared in collaboration with each of these able scholars.

Where heavy reliance was put on condensation from *Regions, Resources, and Economic Growth* – and particularly Chapters 5, 6, 7, and 8 – this extremely demanding task was carried out by Vera Dodds. Also, whatever readability this book has is owed in large measure to Mrs. Dodds' efforts. As in the larger study, able statistical assistance was provided by Erna J. Peters.

Harvey S. Perloff
Director of Regional Studies
Resources for the Future, Inc.

1. Changing Patterns of Regional Growth: A Look at the Growth Figures, 1870-1960

It is a paradox that in the richest country in the world, even at prosperity peaks, there is everywhere deep concern about local economic situations. In the older sections of the United States one finds concern about outmigration of industries and depressed areas. In regions where agriculture is important, the tremendous structural changes that have been taking place, with the widespread decline of rural communities, provide cause for worry about the future. In some of the regions, as in the Far West and in the Southwest, concern about the future of major industries is interspersed with worries about the staggering problem of very rapid end-on-end urban growth. A striking manifestation of the force of local changes under way is the fact that, despite a tremendous amount of national population growth during the decade of the 1950's, approximately half the counties of the country lost population.

In a sense, the uncertainty surrounding regional economic development is comparable to that which attached to the problem of severe business cycle fluctuations over many decades until the relatively successful economic adjustment following World War II. While the problems of economic stabilization are far from solved, the nation has come to have greater assurance in its ability to cope with them. The extreme uncertainties concerning business cycle stabilization have been mitigated as we have come to understand the problems better, have developed techniques for constant metering of business cycle movements, and have evolved more powerful tools for dealing with these problems. This is far from the case with regard to secular problems of development on the regional level. Here there is less knowledge and less assurance, and any sense of assurance will remain lacking until we as a nation develop instrumentalities – public and private, federal, state, and local — adequate to cope with regional and local situations of endless variety and complexity.

Thus far, major national and state concern has centered largely on the depressed areas, on the individual pockets of distress. There is a clear logic to this for both humanitarian and political reasons. However, it is essential to come to realize that this is the pathology of the body economic — the end result and symptom of imbalance and inadequate adjustment. Attention to pathology alone is not enough. It seems evident that in the field of regional economic development our concern increasingly must turn to questions of prevention, rather than cure alone, and to an attempt to understand the type of total environment required for healthy regional development.

Economic developments in every part of the United States have always been dominated by national forces, and yet the growth of the various regions has not proceeded uniformly, but at markedly divergent rates. Why is this so?

This book outlines something of what is known about the complex process of regional economic growth. First, are examined, in order to set the stage, the broad shifts in population and in economic activities along with changes in levels of living during the period from 1870 to 1960. A more detailed study of changes in the regional substructure of the national economy for the recent period 1939-58 follows. The explanation of what is behind these changes is reserved for later chapters.

Indicators of Economic "Growth"

Economic growth has many facets. Inherent in the use of the term is some sense of significant changes in the way people produce, consume, work, live, and play. To record and measure the vast mosaic of change for the nation and its regions is not simple. It is the better part of wisdom to appreciate that existing conceptual and statistical tools can grasp only the crudest notion of the nature and direction of these changes.

A useful starting point is to make a distinction between changes associated with individual and family *welfare* and those associated with the *volume* of economic activities. The most commonly employed measures – really, crude indicators – of economic welfare, of improvement or decline in the average economic status of families and individuals, are the relative levels of per capita real income and the changes in these levels. Different measures are needed in evaluating growth or decline in the *volume* of economic activities – the "more and bigger" aspect of economic growth as against the "better" aspect. Regional growth in volume might be appropriately measured by increases in population, increases in total employment, and/or increases in total income produced or received within a given area.[1]

Population Growth Since 1870

We can get a picture of the different rates of regional development in the United States by tracing the key indices of growth over a relatively long period of time and for large sections of the country. The period covered here is 1870 to 1960 and the regions chosen for study are eight multi-state regions of the continental United States with relatively similar historical-cultural backgrounds.[2] They correspond to those used by the U. S. Department of Commerce in presenting its state personal income estimates (see Figure 1).

Over the ninety-year period, 1870-1960, the population of the continental United States (the 48 states) grew more than fourfold, from 40 million to more than 178 million. From the beginning, the extension of population and economic activity into "newer" areas as well as the relative transformation of "older" and more developed regions have proceeded at quite different rates. Some of the transformation was due to varying local effects of business fluctuations, war, and public policies, but most stemmed from the spread of pro-

[1]The distinction between "welfare" measures and "volume" measures of growth is important because an area may have an increase in one without a corresponding increase in the other. In other words, an area may have an increase in population without an increase in average real per capita income; or an area may have a decrease in the volume of economic activities and in population and yet enjoy an increase in average levels of living.

[2]The eight regions, and states in each, are: *New England*, composed of Maine, New Hampshire, Vermont, Massachusetts, Rhode Island, Connecticut; *Middle Atlantic*, New York, New Jersey, Pennsylvania, Delaware, Maryland, and the District of Columbia; *Great Lakes*, Ohio, Indiana, Illinois, Michigan, Wisconsin; *Southeast*, Virginia, West Virginia, North Carolina, South Carolina, Georgia, Florida, Kentucky, Tennessee, Alabama, Mississippi, Arkansas, Louisiana; *Plains*, Minnesota, Iowa, Missouri, North Dakota, South Dakota, Nebraska, Kansas; *Southwest*, Oklahoma, Texas, New Mexico, Arizona; *Mountain*, Montana, Idaho, Wyoming, Colorado, Utah; and *Far West*, Washington, Oregon, California, Nevada.

Figure 1
Regional Percentage Distribution of U. S. Population – 1870, 1910, and 1960

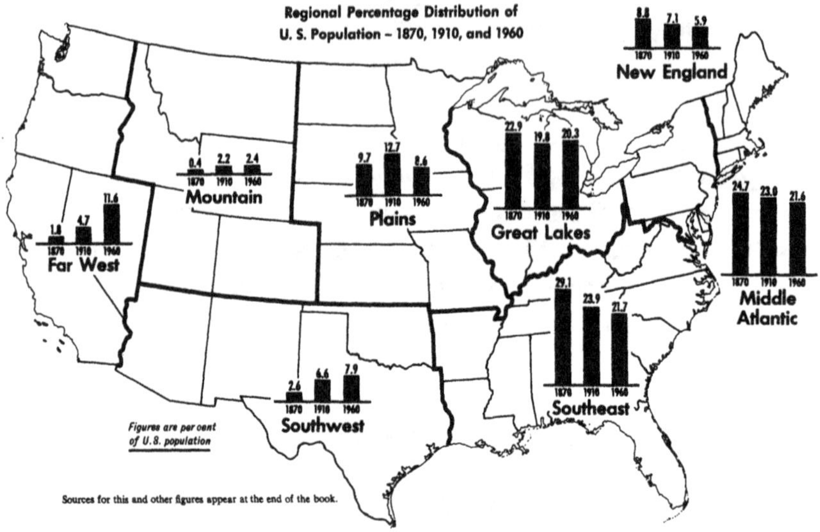

Sources for this and other figures appear at the end of the book.

ductive people and capital into relatively underdeveloped areas in response to new opportunities opening up in various parts of the country.

The movement of population and of economic activities across the United States since 1870 has been a "spreading out" and "filling in" almost like the movement of flood waters coursing over rugged terrain. The most striking feature of this picture has been the phenomenal growth of the West where population almost doubled in relative terms between 1870 and 1910, going from 14.5 per cent of the national total in the earlier date to 26.2 per cent forty years later; by 1960 the Western proportion was 30.5 per cent. But along with the movement West there has been great and intensive development in the older settled regions of the East.

It is worth noting that while the relative rates of increase were highest in the Mountain, Southwest, and Far West regions, the *absolute* increases in population numbers were heaviest in the Southeast, Great Lakes, and Middle Atlantic regions throughout the period so that the great bulk of the population has continued to cluster in areas east of the Mississippi River. Between 1870 and 1960, the Eastern regions gained 90 million persons while the Western regions increased by 49 million. The East contained 85.5 per cent of the nation's population in 1870, 73.8 per cent in 1910, and 69.5 per cent in 1960.

In other words, the peopling of the West since 1870 has cost the four Eastern regions some 16 percentage points of their share of the nation's total population, and since 1910, it is particularly worth noting, only about 4 percentage points. The Great Lakes region, in fact, has a slightly larger proportion of the nation's present population than it had in 1910. The region which secured the greatest share of the *relative* population losses of the East (and of the Plains region as well) was the Far West. Its share of the national population increased from 4.7 per cent to 11.6 per cent of the total between 1910 and 1960.

If regional growth is measured in terms of employed labor force rather than population, almost exactly the same pattern emerges. Between 1870 and 1960 the greatest relative expansion took place in the Far West, Southwest, and Mountain regions; the least in the Southeast and New England. Shares of the national labor force compare quite closely with the population shares for all regions, the greatest deviation being in the Southeast which has been affected by high birth rates and a relatively large proportion of children below working age.

Throughout the period under review there has been a nation-wide decline in the proportion of population living in rural areas and a great increase in urban population. The decline in the share of labor force engaged in resource activities (agriculture, forestry, mining, and fishing) is traced in later chapters, as are the large increases in manufacturing and service employment. At this point it is only necessary to note the profound effect the changing structure of economic activities has had on the urban-rural pattern of population and in turn on the regional pattern of settlement.

It is seen in Table 1 that in 1870 only the New England and Middle Atlantic regions had achieved a relatively high degree of urbanization. By 1910, when the country was almost equally divided between rural and urban populations, four of the eight regions had already achieved a high degree of urbanization, one was approaching the national average, whereas three of the regions still remained largely rural and agricultural. After the turn of the century, manufacturing activities had become significant in the Far West (particularly the coast area) and in the Great Lakes region. Both of these

Table 1. Urban population as percentage of total population, by region, 1870, 1910, 1950, and 1960

Region	1870		1910		1950[a]			1960[b]	
	Total population (thousands)	Per cent urban	Total population (thousands)	Per cent urban	Total population (thousands)	Per cent urban: Old definition	Per cent urban: New definition	Total population (thousands)	Per cent urban
United States	39,818	25.2	91,972	45.7	150,697	59.0	64.0	178,464	69.9
New England	3,488	*44.4*	6,553	*73.3*	9,315	*74.3*	*76.0*	10,509	*76.6*
Middle Atlantic	9,848	*44.1*	21,145	*70.2*	33,627	*74.0*	*80.0*	38,479	*80.8*
Great Lakes	9,124	21.6	18,251	*52.7*	30,399	*65.7*	*69.6*	36,225	*72.9*
Southeast	11,600	9.5	22,007	19.4	33,789	42.5	42.5	38,754	52.1
Plains	3,857	18.9	11,638	33.2	14,061	49.9	52.1	15,395	58.8
Southwest	1,012	6.9	6,085	22.5	11,375	55.5	58.8	14,161	*72.4*
Mountain	171	13.9	2,020	40.7	3,484	51.8	55.9	4,317	65.0
Far West	718	*31.2*	4,274	*56.0*	14,647	*62.7*	*74.9*	20,624	*81.6*

[a] For comparison, "per cent urban in 1950" is given in terms of both old and new census definitions of urban population. The new definition adopted in 1950 comprises all persons living in (a) incorporated cities, boroughs, towns (except where these are simply minor civil divisions of counties), and villages, of 2,500 inhabitants or more; (b) the densely settled urban fringe around cities of 50,000 or more; and (c) unincorporated places of 2,500 inhabitants or more outside any urban fringe. The "old" definition limited urban population to all persons living in incorporated places of 2,500 inhabitants or more and in areas classified as urban under special rules relating to population sizes and density.

[b] The 1960 total population and percentage urban exclude Alaska (226,000, 38.1 per cent) and Hawaii (633,000, 76.5 per cent).

Note: Figures in italics are above the national average.

Sources for this and other tables appear at the end of the book.

regions, following the lead of New England and the Middle Atlantic states, had begun to develop extensive "systems" of cities – great urban masses highlighting the key manufacturing zones of the nation. By 1960, every region had more urban than rural population and economic growth had become essentially an urban phenomenon.

Growth in Total Personal Income

A comprehensive and suggestive measure of regional economic growth is provided by total personal income. If we examine data showing changes in the regional distribution of the nation's total personal income between 1880 (the first date for which such statistics are available) and 1960, what appears is an over-all pattern of different rates of regional growth not too dissimilar from that shown by the data on population increase. Like changes in population, the changes in income reflect the impressive growth in the volume of economic activities in the Far West and Southwest regions, the gradual decline in relative shares of the New England and Middle Atlantic regions, and the long-term stability of the Great Lakes region. But a closer look at the data reveals that the distribution of total income among the various regions does not correspond to the population distribution because of considerable differences in income-earning capacity among the regions. The Southeast, for example, in 1880 had 27 per cent of the nation's population but less than 14 per cent of the total national income; by 1959-60, with roughly 22 per cent of the total population, it had 16 per cent of the total national income.

Per Capita Income

The critical interplay between population growth and growth in total income is reflected in the *per capita* income levels and in the rates of increase in these levels as among the various regions. Table 2 shows estimates of changes in real income per capita (1959 dollars) over the 1880-1959 period in each of the regions. These data show a marked tendency for regional per capita incomes to become more nearly equal as the regions became economically more interdependent and the nation politically less "sectional." In 1880, regional averages ranged from a high of 211 per cent of the national average (in the

Table 2. Regional real income per capita, 1880, 1920, 1940, and 1959, and as percentage of national average

(Weighted average of state incomes per capita, 1959 dollars)

Region	1880		1920		1940		1959	
	Per capita income	Per cent	Per capita income	Per cent	Per capita income	Per cent	Per capita income	Per cent
United States	$ 592.4	100.0	$1,133.3	100.0	$1,370.9	100.0	$2,166	100.0
New England	*833.3*	140.7	*1,410.3*	124.4	*1,744.2*	127.2	*2,396*	110.6
Middle Atlantic	*829.0*	140.0	*1,514.6*	133.2	*1,820.2*	132.8	*2,540*	117.3
Great Lakes	*602.7*	101.8	*1,222.5*	107.9	*1,536.8*	112.1	*2,337*	107.9
Southeast	295.3	49.9	639.6	56.4	790.3	57.6	1,565	72.3
Plains	531.7	89.8	982.3	86.7	1,112.9	81.2	1,978	91.3
Southwest	358.2	60.5	914.1	80.7	963.1	70.2	1,887	87.1
Mountain	*983.3*	166.0	*1,158.2*	102.2	1,223.5	89.2	1,990	91.9
Far West	*1,251.3*	211.3	*1,530.5*	135.1	*1,808.7*	131.9	*2,565*	118.4

Note: Figures in italics are above the national average.

Far West where 2 per cent of the national population lived unusually well) to a low of 50 per cent (in the Southeast which had 29 per cent of the total population). By 1959, the same high- and low-income regions had drawn much closer together in terms of relative averages, with the Far West (with 12 per cent of the population) having an income level 118 per cent of the national average and the Southeast (with 22 per cent of the population) showing 72 per cent of the national average income.

Since 1920, regions in which manufacturing and service activities predominated have had considerably higher incomes than the less industrialized Mountain, Plains, Southwest, and Southeast regions. Before 1920, the income advantage of the more urban-industrialized regions was not always so consistent. In fact, in the two decades just before 1900, the Far West and Mountain regions, with their sparse population sharing the regions' proportionately high total personal income, had the highest income per capita in the country; and it was only after 1900 that the industrial areas maintained a consistently higher-than-average position in the nation's income structure. First the Middle Atlantic and New England regions, followed after World War I by the Great Lakes region, closed the gap between their income levels and those of the Far West. Between 1920 and 1940, the Middle Atlantic region was the pace-setter for the nation. Since 1920, there has been little change in the relative per capita income position of the various regions.

To sum up, with minor qualifications and at varying rates of speed, per capita incomes everywhere have been converging toward the national level. Adjustments between population and income-earning opportunities have worked especially well in filling in the "newer" Western regions and in maintaining a large and growing population in the well-established industrial areas of the country. Unfortunately, adjustments that would bring the regions that are much poorer in per capita income close to the national average have not occurred quite as readily.

2. Factors Behind the Volume Growth of Regions

What is behind the different rates at which regions tend to grow? This is clearly a complicated matter, but in order to clarify the forces at work the key variables can be grouped into the following four sets of factors, all of them interrelated through the workings of the market mechanism or price system:

1. The key national, and in some instances international, factors; these are the "change-initiating forces" which influence the volume and composition of regional (and national) economic activity – changes in taste, income distribution, technology, governmental policy, and organization.
2. The requirements of the major industries and the factors behind their locational and production decisions.
3. The factors behind the job and consumption decisions of individuals and families.
4. The nature of the individual regions, including such factors as resource endowment, levels of skills of the labor force, internal market size, and other factors which add up to what might be called the "relative cumulative advantage" of each region.

National Change-Initiating Forces

The secular and cyclical forces of the closely knit national economy have an important effect on economic developments in every part of the United States. The rates at which new plants are built, and new job opportunities occur, the expansion and contraction of governmental activities – these and related factors have a direct bearing on the rate of growth in various parts of the country.

The factors influencing the character of national economic growth also influence the patterns of regional growth. Here, those change-initiating forces that are directly related to the growth of specific industries play a large role. As a family's income rises, the family spends its additional income on a greater variety of goods than was possible with its former income. Expenditures for automobiles, household equipment, travel, and recreation, for instance, are expanded much more than expenditures for food and clothing. This pattern of demand, or "income elasticity of demand," as it is known, interacts with the supply pattern in influencing the composition of total production and the relative price changes among commodities. Hence, in the normal course of events, as per capita income grows, relatively more of society's total resources are devoted to the production of such items as automobiles and relatively less to producing food.

Similarly, the effects of technological change, particularly on productivity, are unevenly distributed. For some products the impact on output and prices may be quite different from the impact on employment. Agriculture is a dramatic example. In this field, increased productivity, resulting from new technology and improved practices, has enabled various sections to produce much greater quantities with fewer workers. Coupled with a low rate of increase in demand for most agricultural products, this has retarded growth in employment in regions where agricultural activities are important.

For the nation as a whole, agriculture's share of the total labor force declined from 26 per cent in 1920 to 12 per cent in 1950. During this period, in the Southeast and Southwest regions where the effects have been particularly marked, agriculture's share of the Southeast region's labor force declined from 50 per cent to 21 per cent, and of the Southwest's from 45 per cent to 16 per cent.

In contrast, some industries, such as many which produce consumer durables and chemical products, have expanded employment as a result of new technology and high rates of increase in demand for their products. Clearly, since these national change-initiating forces operate differently for different commodities and since the regions differ widely in their patterns of production, some regions will be stimulated to rapid growth while others will be little affected.

Transportation costs within and among regions also are affected by forces at the national level. Truck and airplane improvements and the development of co-ordinated container transport by truck, rail, or barge, for example, can influence the production and location decisions of industries. The impact upon regions varies with the degree to which their industries are dependent upon transportation as a factor in production or marketing.

Changes in the characteristics of the national population can further influence the growth of a region. For example, the rising average age of the population accompanied by an extended pension system means that many more people are freed from motives of job-seeking when moving from one area to another. And this, in turn, leads to significant changes in the size of markets and in supply of labor in the various regions.

Acting as "transmission agents" between the national forces and the individual regions are the various industry groups and individuals or family units. These are the key decision-making entities determining the economic changes within and among regions.

The principles that govern the location of economic activities are no different from those governing all of man's efforts to make the most of his economic resources. On the production side of the balance sheet, expenditures for "inputs" reflect an effort to produce with the smallest possible commitment of economic resources the kind of product-mix buyers want most. On the consumption side, expenditures for products reflect the desire to acquire a market basket of items that will provide the greatest satisfaction possible within the constraints of individual incomes. The complex set of decisions that constitute man's economizing effort is made largely within the framework of the market mechanism.

The Location of Productive Activities[1]

The businessman's main concern in picking a production site is to select one which will enable him to operate at the most profitable level. Production costs and revenues differ from one site to another, depending upon variations in access to the basic inputs and markets that are significant for the specific activities. Sometimes input access is dominant in determining the location of an activity, and sometimes market access; sometimes neither is dominant, with the result that

[1]Here "productive" is used in its broadest sense, to include all extractive, processing, trade, and service activities that contribute to economic welfare.

the location will be intermediate or indeterminate. This has led economists to characterize production activity as being input-oriented, market-oriented, oriented to intermediate sites, or, when none of these applies, as "foot-loose."

The "primary" activities – farming, mining, forestry, and fishing – are of course largely oriented to natural resources inputs. The location of "secondary" activities – those having to do with all forms of manufacture – can be dominated by factors of proximity either to markets or to raw or semi-processed inputs. "Tertiary," or service activities, dealing as they do with such functions as transportation and communications, construction, trade, finance, government, the professions, and recreation, are by and large closely tied to markets.

The foregoing three groupings comprise all economic activity. But there are innumerable permutations in the factors governing the location choice of an *individual* activity or industry within any one of the three groups. Food processing, for example, is often best undertaken close to the site of the crops or livestock the industry utilizes. This is true also of the production of fertilizers and tin cans. Some manufacturing activities, such as certain kinds of apparel manufacture, and many of the service activities tend to be labor-oriented. Sometimes the location of a *specialized* type of labor or management resource may be the determining location factor.

Market orientation may also be of different types. Many market-oriented activities – for example, the production of bakery goods and consumer services – are oriented to final, or consumer, markets. Certain others, whose functions require processed or semi-processed materials – machine shops, wholesaling, and automobile production, for example – are linked to both markets and inputs and are therefore intermediate in orientation. Petroleum refining and certain petrochemical industries have mixed orientation patterns: under one combination of markets and inputs, they tend to be market-oriented; another combination may lead to input orientation. It is important to realize, also, that any given production activity might have a different locational orientation at the same time in different regions; differences in the cost of labor is one reason for this.

Some activities, such as hosiery production or some branches of electronics, have no strong locational orientation pattern. They may be foot-loose in varying degrees when deciding on the location of a plant. Industries of this type and industries which must attract a special type of labor force that is in short supply tend to place emphasis on attractive living conditions.

Except in those unusual cases in which location is either fixed or entirely indeterminate, transfer costs – the cost of transporting unfinished goods for final processing or finished products to final markets – affect an industry's choice of location. Their influence can be operative even where inputs or outputs are immobile or where substitute sources exist for the same inputs or substitute markets for the same output. Mining activities, for example, are inevitably oriented to the immobile natural site of the resource. But among alternatives, the site selected will be one which offers the best total access to the essential resource input *and* its potential markets. In situations like this, the transfer alternatives offered are a major factor in determining the order in which resource sites are brought to use and the intensity with which they are exploited.

For the majority of enterprises, however, production inputs and outputs are mobile and substitutable and transfer relations are important. Thus many areas in the economic landscape would seem to be potential production sites. In reality, however, certain factors limit the sites that are to be considered. When, for example, an industry can produce economically only on a large scale, such "internal" scale economies leading to firms of large size have the effect of reducing the number of feasible input sources (in the case of input orientation) or markets (in the case of market orientation).

As a case in point, if a firm is market-oriented it must have a market large enough to permit the operation of at least one minimum-sized efficient plant. Considerations of "external" scale economies (arising from the proximity of other firms whose products are tied in varying ways to the production of the specific firm) will also exert an influence upon locational patterns. Or, a firm may weigh heavily the availability of certain specialized services, which enables it to turn over to specialized concerns part of its calculating, planning, or technological functions. External cost savings due to the availability of *general* types of services (e.g., maintenance, banking, or business services) may also be important, as may be a ready supply of variously skilled labor or of community services such as power and water or other "overhead" items. These savings in external costs lead to agglomerations of industries and services which depend upon one another for their continued productivity.

Since these agglomeration economies tend to coincide with high population concentrations, and hence markets, their effect often is to strengthen existing tendencies to market orientation—and the piling up of more agglomeration upon existing agglomeration. The tremendous growth of our metropolitan centers and the growth of the Manufacturing Belt—continuing in spite of the spreading out of manufacturing activity across the country—can largely be explained in these terms. (The Manufacturing Belt covers roughly the Northeast, Middle Atlantic, and Great Lakes regions, *excluding* northern New England.)

The importance of intermediate inputs, such as partially manufactured products, of markets, and of scale economies suggests why the *existing* distribution of population and economic activities among and within the regions is itself a factor in the differing patterns of regional growth. The current agglomerations or concentrations, which are essentially the end-result of past growth, are themselves a significant influence of future growth. This is so because the overwhelming majority of locational decisions must take market, input, and transfer factors *as given*. Thus, the decision of the present, or the "marginal" decision, is based to an important extent on the locational (and price) situation as it has evolved from the past. This is not to suggest that for the firm making a location or production decision the future is not the key consideration, but simply that at any point in time future costs and returns must necessarily be estimated in terms of the relatively slowly evolving national pattern of agglomeration.

Whenever there is initiation of a productive operation within a region in response to external and internal demand, fixed capital is invested. The rate at which this capital can be depreciated profitably often controls its continued use in the region, even if opportunities for new capital investment with higher rates of return develop elsewhere. Once an investment is made in plant and equipment, it usually pays a firm to continue operations within the existing location for a relatively long period of time.

The same general considerations apply to the "investment" of workers in their chosen location. In part, the investment may be in fixed capital in the home and in part it is a social investment involving close bonds to friends, ties to children's schools, and the comfort and security of the familiar scene. There is some analogy here with industry's fixed capital investment. An older person, like an older firm, will weigh alternative opportunities differently than will a younger person.

While the relatively inflexible elements which reflect the "sunk" costs must be given adequate consideration, there are also significant elements of flexibility in the economic system, and these are of particular importance in analyzing different rates of economic growth. Capital (and particularly "new capital") as well as labor (and, again, particularly "new labor") do tend to seek new and better opportunities and will move over wide areas of the country in an attempt to improve their over-all situation. Free trade among the regions can be expected to work strongly towards a geographic equalization of the prices of the factors of production—or, at least, towards a narrowing of the spread in prices—through its effect on the relative demands for the different factors.

We have already seen that regions do not necessarily maintain a given position in the total scheme of things over long periods of time. A major reason is that the requirements of the individual industries are constantly subject to change and therefore the advantages or disadvantages of a region will be weighed quite differently over time. Some of these changing requirements are dramatic in their effects; others are more subtle. Nevertheless, these slower-paced changes can over time have a powerful influence on the regions within which the different activities tend to expand their production. Mechanization of cotton cultivation, for example, has enabled the cotton industry to produce a crop far more economically in large flat areas than on smaller hilly sites. This has contributed to the move of cotton to the flat lands of the Southwest and its relative decline in the hilly sections of the Southeast.

The relative *rates* at which individual industries grow over a period of time also influence the patterns of regional growth. Clearly, a region which contains a rapidly growing industry will receive thereby an acceleration in growth. However, two factors should be considered if this element is to be properly weighed. First, what is meant by an "industry"? The same term is used to cover a hierarchical set of establishments. Thus, every "industry" can be broken down into smaller and smaller classes, as when the "manufacturing industry" is broken down into food processing, chemicals, rubber, leather, machinery, etc., and these in turn are broken down into subcategories, and on down the line. (The Census Bureau recognizes this by defining "industries" in terms of 1-digit classes, 2-digit classes, etc., until in some cases 5- and 6-digit classes are reached.) Some of the subcategories of an industry will normally be expanding even if the average for the whole group shows a decline. This is the case, for example, with the growing cattle industry in the generally declining over-all industry of agriculture; conversely, the textile industry is a declining subcategory of the generally growing manufacturing category.

The second factor is the obverse of the first. A region may grow by getting an increasing proportion of an industry that over-all is declining nationally. This would be the case when the remaining portions of a declining industry all cluster into a region, which gains in volume with regard to this industry while all other regions are losing out. This is an important explanation of the rapid growth of certain regions identified in later pages as "growth regions."

When these various possibilities are combined, it can be seen that a region may contain, at one extreme, an increasing share of the growing subcategory of a nationally increasing industry or, at the opposite extreme, a declining share of a declining subcategory of a nationally declining industry—and there are many combinations in between. Regional economic growth can be understood only when all these elements are clarified, measured, and explained.

Consumption Activities

Since, from the worker's viewpoint, access to varied means of employment is usually a necessity, it follows that the population is distributed essentially on the basis of regional distribution of economic opportunity. Therefore, it would seem that the factors explaining the location of production activity would also explain the distribution of consumption activity. But this is not entirely so. For one thing, some 9 per cent of the population is over 65 years of age. Of these people, approximately two-thirds are not working and, because most of their consumption requirements can be met equally well in all regions, many are free to seek out the more intangible advantages, such as attractions of climate and seashore, which vary substantially from region to region. A further group of people, although employed, may choose to live in areas relatively distant from their work in order to enjoy the amenities they consider important. Adding to these factors the tendency of certain "foot-loose" firms to seek locations that are attractive to their specialized type of labor force, one can find three reasons why the role of "independent" household decisions should not be overlooked in analyzing the distribution of population. Particularly affected are areas like Florida, California, and parts of the Southwest and Mountain regions.

It is not surprising to find that the most rapid economic growth in recent decades has taken place in precisely those areas where both the consumption and production elements are relatively favorable and reinforce each other.

The Nature of Regions: Relative Advantages and Disadvantages

Certain industries contribute more to regional growth than others. Certain industries pay higher wages than others. Some are physically more attractive than the average. But not all regions have the relative advantages that attract such industries. Many can expect to grow only slowly on the basis of the industries for which they do have special advantages. This is another way of saying that not every area can hope to have the clean, fast-growing electronic and research industries it desires. Looked at in terms of relative advantages in resources, markets, human skills and labor costs, amenities, climate, and transport facilities and cost, some areas can hope to grow mainly by attracting labor-intensive industries; others, by attracting certain kinds of processing industries using relatively unexploited natural resources; some may have special advantages for certain types of assembly operations; still others for relatively intensive recreation activities, and so on.

The attraction of industry is clearly a competitive matter. There are many things that a region can do to enhance its locational advantages, particularly with regard to facilities, as in improving transportation, and major services, such as better education. But many features of nature and position within the nation are unalterable, and so a realistic appraisal of a region's relative advantages and disadvantages with regard to *input-output access* is an essential starting point for understanding its growth potential, as well as its past growth.

When one speaks of "access" as the sum of the relative advantages and disadvantages for the production of a particular commodity *at some given place,* more is implied than just the resistance, and hence costs, imposed by distance on the assembly of inputs and the distribution of outputs. The question of *relative* costs is critical; a favorable opportunity at a given place might not be exploited because of the existence of a better opportunity elsewhere. Therefore, "rivalry" and "opportunity" costs are important in the concept of access, as is the opportunity for new investment. Decisions on new investment are determined by relations at the margin—that is, by small increments of change rather than by average relationships. Thus, it is quite possible that an area might have, on the average, favorable conditions for the production of a given commodity and yet not grow, simply because the opportunities for new investment are not quite as favorable in this area *relative* to other areas.

When regions are examined in terms of costs and markets, or *input-output access,* with regard to the requirements of specific industries and for all economic activities taken together, the extent to which they vary in their prospects for growth becomes apparent. The sixteen conceptual regions shown in Figure 2, oversimplified as they may be, serve to focus attention on the range of possible growth, and point up, for example, the fallacy of the extreme local economic-development approach which can lead to regard every region and community as capable of limitless economic expansion.

To the extent that a region's general access characteristics may be taken as a rough index of its potential for growth, Region 4 in Figure 2 would have little prospect for growth, while Region 13 would have an unsurpassed growth potential. Other regions fall in between these extremes. Regions 1, 2, 3, 8, 12, and 16 are only a little better off than 4. In these cases, reasonable access to inputs is offset by lack of market access—i.e., limited markets within easy reach—or vice versa. Thus, for example, one type of region may be developed to the extent that it contains an important mineral resource which is much in demand, but its development may be essentially limited to the exploitation of that particular mineral because of its disadvantage with regard to transporting almost all other products to distant markets. In general, regions 6, 7, 10, and 11 are somewhat better off because they at least have some access to both inputs and

Figure 2

A Schematic Presentation of Types of Regions That Can Exhibit Different Growth Potentials

		Good access to basic inputs* from external regional and national sources		Poor access to basic inputs* from external regional and national sources	
		Good access to basic inputs in home region	Poor access to basic inputs in home region	Good access to basic inputs in home region	Poor access to basic inputs in home region
Poor access to external regional and national markets	Poor access to markets in home region	#1 II	#2 I	#3 I	#4 0
	Good access to markets in home region	#5 III	#6 II	#7 II	#8 I
Good access to external regional and national markets	Poor access to markets in home region	#9 III	#10 II	#11 II	#12 I
	Good access to markets in home region	#13 IV	#14 III	#15 III	#16 II

*Not only basic resources but important intermediate sources need to be considered.

NOTE: Roman numerals indicate number of "good" access dimensions, and suggest relative over-all locational advantages or disadvantages.

markets. Regions 5, 9, 14, and 15 are still better off because they have advantages either in large home markets or good access to national markets combined with advantages in acquiring inputs or in shipping out their products or both.

The restraints placed upon the future prospects for these regions also differ. Region 4 would have dim prospects of evolving into a region type with greater growth potential. Any change in its character must rest upon a doubly fortuitous set of circumstances. Technology, discovery, or institutional changes must bring about an improvement in its access to both inputs and markets. For Region 3, which has good access to inputs in the home region but no external markets, the prognosis is poor but not as hopeless. This region must either overcome the restriction upon its transfer relationships with other regions, or exploit its resources through a prolonged series of internal growth sequences. Region 12, with good access to external markets but poor access to input sources, might have a better prospect for breaking out of its dilemma. Discovery, technology, or even the pressure of growing demand might improve its access to basic inputs.

In weighing the growth prospects of a region, its present production characteristics or state of development are of course significant, but they do not entirely determine the course of future growth. Consider the direction of growth sequences. Development is generally thought to follow a prescribed sequence, with growth initiated by advances in primary extractive activity, followed by the development of more and more complex manufacturing, and followed in turn by more and more advanced servicing activities. But when one considers the variety of growth experiences suggested in Figure 4, it is evident that this is not always the case for the regions of an economically advanced nation.

A region such as type 11 might show a sequence of development completely the reverse of the sequence typically hypothesized. Florida is an example. It has had a limited scope for development on the basis of the size of the home market and relatively poor access to external input sources. The major characteristic of its input access in the home region has been its coast and agreeable climate. Its access to external markets for this resource was good because, in our highly developed economy, population movements often take the form of a quest for amenities rather than economic opportunity. The exploitation of a resource was dominant in this development, but it is a special kind of resource that might be identified as a resource-service. No primary activities in the old sense were associated with its exploitation. Rather, the exploitation of this resource required an intense development of tertiary activities which service population. In 1950, some 66 per cent of all employment in Florida was in the service activities. Market-oriented activities dominated.

With steadily mounting population—from 1,836,000 in 1939 to 4,442,000 in 1958—a stage is developing where the availability of business services in Florida is attracting increasing quantities of secondary manufacturing activities. Typical of these are small-scale, market-oriented manufacturing, such as metal construction products, and relatively foot-loose activities such as electronics. As the wealth and size of the population grows, deficit food supplies make possible the use of agricultural lands which at an earlier date could not be considered a significant economic resource. This calls for an expansion in the primary sector of the economy. In this situation the tertiary-secondary-primary sequence is more logical than the reverse.

A growth sequence may possibly start in the "middle" and perhaps go both ways. A region of type 6 or 8 might exhibit this kind of sequence. Sometimes the exhaustion of a resource or the development of a substitute may leave a region "overdeveloped." If labor is slow in moving out, the pool of relatively immobile labor with depressed wages may attract secondary manufacturing activities oriented to cheap labor—as has been happening in the Appalachian mining areas. The new secondary activity may induce growth sequences that lead to expansion in primary, tertiary, and other secondary activities. If this should happen, the region *may* regain a level of growth and production commensurate with that of other regions.

The variety of growth experience is apparent not only in the different sequences that are possible but also in the variety of functional pathways it might take. For a region (such as 7) with good access to inputs and markets only in the home region, growth is largely restricted to the internal evolution of specialization characteristic of more or less "closed" regions. In another region (such as 11) growth may take the form of interregional specialization in response to external stimulation. In other regions (such as 13) it is more apt to be compounded of elements of both external and internal response. A region (such as 10) which has poor access to inputs and markets in the home region might sustain considerable growth because of its *nodal,* or strategic, position with reference to external sources and markets.

Regions vary widely in their capacity to achieve mature development. A rationalized, variegated, mature development of economic functions is unlikely in a region that does not have good access to large external national markets. All of the functions that are dominated by important external and internal scale economies would be denied to it. Such a region may have to continue its development through more limited specialized activities. Given sensible policies (and good luck) its people may enjoy high levels of living, but substantial growth in volume would be unlikely.

"Export" and "Internal" Determinants of Regional Growth

One way of looking at the mechanics of regional growth, as already suggested, is in terms of the "internal" characteristics of the region as well as of its attractiveness for *export* industries, whose products are intended mainly for markets outside the region. A region's growth typically has been promoted by its ability to produce export goods or services at a competitive advantage with respect to other regions. The ability to export induces a flow of income into the region which tends to expand its internal markets for both national and region-serving goods and services. The extent of this so-called multiplier effect is related to certain internal features that characterize the economic and social structure of the region. Regions tend to differ substantially in the degree of development that becomes associated with the growth of the export industries and in what happens to the income that flows in from the export sales.

Some of these internal features are related to the nature of the export industries and particularly to the localized industrial linkages; services attaching to the export sector are also important here. Thus, the shipment of heavy export products from a region may influence the development of substantial transportation facilities and services within the region. The manufacture of machinery often brings a variety of servicing operations into being; so does the manufacture of style goods.

The quantity and type of labor required by the export industries and the relative levels of wages paid has, of course, an obvious relationship to a region's internal development. Another important feature is the income distribution that tends to be associated with a given type of regional export product. A dramatic example here is the contrast between the nineteenth century plantation system in the Southeast, with its highly unequal distribution of income from the production of cotton and tobacco—and the extremely limited local markets that developed—compared with the independent-farmer production system of the Midwest with its broad income base and its growing markets for local goods and services.

Internal regional development takes the form both of internal structural changes (such as an increase in the proportion of the labor force employed in "advanced" manufacturing and service industries) and an expansion of the local market for all sorts of goods and services. As the regional market expands and region-serving activities proliferate, conditions may develop for *self-reinforcing* regional growth, and new internal factors may become important in determining the rates of regional growth. This happens when more and more industries are attracted by the external economies associated with social overhead capital and the agglomeration of industries, as well as by the desired internal economies of scale which can be achieved when producing through a branch plant on a large enough scale.

This phenomenon can be seen when tracing the economic development of a state like California. The occurrence of rapid self-sustaining growth involves a shift in the relative importance of growth factors—away from the dominance of the export sector and in the direction of the internal organization of production—which makes it possible for the region to play a more elaborate role in the national economy.

The export and internal determinants of regional economic expansion can be brought together in the concept of *cumulative advantage.* It is cumulative advantage, and not an unusual advantage in any one aspect, which is determining of over-all sustained economic growth. In the development of the United States economy the role of cumulative advantage is most clearly seen in the remarkable growth of the Middle Atlantic region and, later, of the Great Lakes region. Both have enjoyed unequaled access to national markets. Each was endowed with unusually good resources and attracted a vigorous, risk-taking group of people who found ever-new ways of exploiting the regions' advantages. A relatively equal distribution of income and other favorable internal factors contributed to the development of huge internal markets, so that export and region-serving activities built on each other stage by stage. It is not surprising that these regions have had great growth over the years, and have enjoyed a considerable degree of permanence in their growth patterns. Where, for example, in 1900 the Manufacturing Belt contained 49 per cent of the nation's population, in 1960 it still had 47 per cent of the population after sixty years of the "movement West." Currently we are seeing the impact of cumulative advantage in a dramatic form in the development of California.

One final note, to stress again the competitive factor. Any advantage which a region may have vis-à-vis other regions is always relative. This is so whether the focus is in terms of input and market advantages in the production of a single product or the products of a single industry, or whether the focus is in terms of cumulative advantages for over-all economic growth. Whether we are looking backward and explaining past growth or looking forward and analyzing potential growth, the view must necessarily be a competitive one. Regional growth is a highly competitive matter in an open economy.

3. Long-Term Changes in the Regional Distribution of Economic Activity

Each region plays a special economic role in the large and open United States economy, and this role changes over time as the national forces influencing supply and demand change and as the characteristics of the regions change. The economic growth of regions is closely tied to these changing relationships. The part each region plays in the United States national scene is very broadly defined by the region's natural resource endowment as well as by its geographic position (especially in relation to major centers of population) and its period of settlement and development.

The contribution of natural resources to the economic development of the regions has been constantly changing because resource endowment is itself an evolving element in the economic picture, closely associated with the dynamics of national economic growth. Resource endowment is related to the determinants of final demand: consumer preferences, income distribution and foreign trade on the one hand, and organization and technology of production on the other. As these variables change, so does the content of resource endowment, and with it the relative advantages among regions supplying material inputs and services for the national economy. There are at least three fairly distinctive stages of change: (1) the early agricultural period, (2) the minerals period spurring the growth of manufacturing, and (3), in a more limited way, the "amenity" resources period which has greatly enlarged the scope of service activities.

The Agricultural Period

From its colonial origins the American economy developed as a producer of resource inputs to the rapidly expanding European economy. To serve such a function the endowment which counted in early America was arable land with its environmental component of climate and water, and this, with access to the growing European market for agricultural staples, set up the conditions for regional growth in early America. As a result, the regional economies developed along certain discernible lines: a deep water port as the nucleus of an agricultural hinterland well adapted for the production of the staple commodity in demand on the world market.

The growth potential of these nucleated regions depended heavily on the extent and richness of the hinterland accessible to the port. Since good agricultural land was almost a free resource while labor and capital were dear, expanded production was effected by bringing more land into production and so extending the limits of the hinterland. The force of the outward push for land is suggested by the fact that population west of the Alleghenies grew from just over 100,000, according to the 1790 Census, to almost 6.5 million in 1840—with more than 87 per cent of the labor force working in agriculture.

The characteristics of this early period, then, can be generalized. (1) The regional endowment that made for growth was "good" land advantageously situated as related to transportation routes to the market centers. (2) The distribution of economic activity in the period before 1840 was essentially a function of the expanding, agricultural regions reaching into the economic vacuum of an unsettled continent to bring ever greater areas of land under cultivation. (3) This resource-dominated expansion of the economy set the stage for the next important development by establishing a geography of markets, transport, and labor force to condition the nature of succeeding growth.

The Influence of Minerals

Somewhere around 1840-50 the next important resource stage began as a result of the emerging importance of minerals in production. The rapid growth of the railroads and the expansion of processing industries resulted in new input requirements. A new set of resources became important and a new set of locational forces came into play. At first this period was dominated by the growing demand for iron and steel and by the rapid elaboration of their production technology. At this point it was the geographical juxtaposition of coal, iron ore, and the market which afforded the great impetus for growth. Unlike agricultural land, minerals were important not only for their direct contribution to regional growth but also for the linkages they established with succeeding stages of production. Iron and steel production, for example, could not be far separated from the sources of mineral inputs. The early concentration of steel-making in western Pennsylvania was a result of these relationships, for this area was well endowed with deposits of iron and coal and was also central to a concentrated market stretching from Boston and New York westward. As the center of gravity of the market shifted west and as Mesabi ores replaced depleted local ores, the iron and steel industries also shifted westward along the southern shores of the Great Lakes.

With the increase in demand for nonferrous metals, depletion of accessible ore deposits in the East, and the railroad's penetration of the West, the role of mineral resources in regional growth began to be continent-wide in scope. In the Mountain region stretching from the Canadian border to the Southwest states, mining of metal ores was the leading factor in economic development. In 1870, when mineral extraction involved 1.5 per cent of the national labor force, it accounted for no less than 26.5 per cent in this region. (It has since declined until in 1950 the proportion was 3.5 per cent – still double the national average.) But except for primary processing of ores, the minerals resource base stimulated comparatively little linked activity in the Mountain states. With most of the weight loss taking place during concentration and smelting, transport of the product was relatively economical and, therefore, the established distribution of the market, chiefly concentrated in the Northeast, governed the location of succeeding stages of metals fabrication.

The years from 1870 to 1910 marked a period of tremendous growth in the output of mineral products: the production of iron ore increased by 1,500 per cent, copper by 2,700 per cent, and lead by 2,000 per cent. In comparison, the next forty years saw relatively modest increases: between 1910 and 1950 iron ore output increased by 115 per cent, copper by 68 per cent, and lead by 12 per cent. It was during the earlier period that the most extensive interregional shifts in production took place.

The data shown in Figure 3 underline the highly selective regional effects resulting from the growth of a minerals-based economy. Between 1870 and 1910, truly huge shifts in copper production took place from the Great Lakes region to the Mountain region, and to a lesser extent to the Southwest and Far West. Throughout the eighty-year period, pig-iron production shifted steadily from the Middle Atlantic states to the Great Lakes, and some of it to the Southeast. Meantime, even though the *relative* importance of agricultural production was declining, significant interregional changes in agriculture were taking place. The shift in wheat production from the Lakes states to the Plains, and later to the other western regions, was as striking as anything that took place in minerals production.

Some notion of the enormous changes in national *requirements* which gave rise to these interregional shifts can be gained by measuring the changes in the composition of the value of purchases (in constant dollars) within the broad mineral categories over the 1870-1950 period. This can be done by estimating the end-of-period totals which would have to be redistributed among the categories of products to recreate the beginning-of-period percentage distribution.

Within the mineral fuels the total shift was equivalent to 57 per cent away from bituminous and anthracite coals and towards petroleum and natural gas fuels — materials which were scarcely considered as resources a decade before 1870. Among the metals the total shift was almost 34 per cent away from iron, lead, and tin in the direction of the light metals and ferro-alloys; and one-fourth of this shift involved such metals as aluminum, manganese, nickel, and molybdenum for which the economy of 1870 had little or no use. Similar information about the nonmetals is limited to the more recent period, between 1910 and 1950, during which time their internal composition shifted by 31 per cent away from stone and towards other construction materials and basic chemical materials. More than one-fourth of the shift was to materials unknown as resources in 1870.

Figure 3
Distribution of Regional Shares of Production, 1870, 1910, 1950

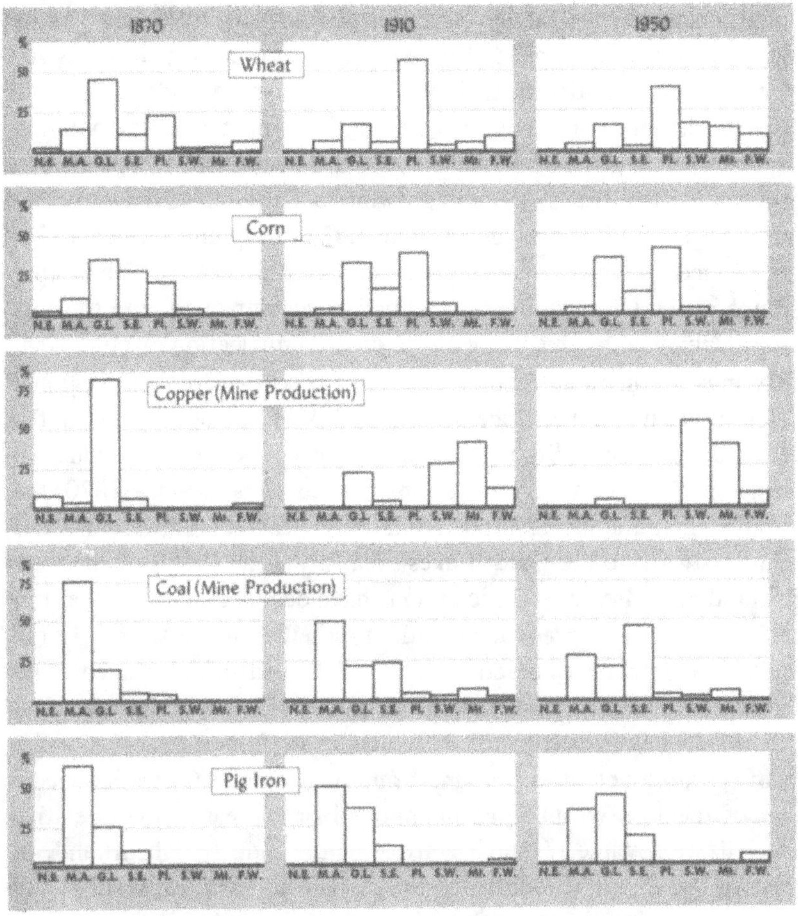

The Manufacturing Heartland and the Resources Regions

During the entire eighty-year period, the changing patterns of resource use conditioned the regional distribution of economic activity. Early in the minerals-dominant era, around the 1850's, the Middle Atlantic region emerged as the core of an "industrial heartland," with southern New England as a smaller eastern partner and with the Great Lakes adjoining on the west. This entire area benefited from the "cumulative advantages" discussed in Chapter 2 – rich resources, growing populations, a well-developed transportation system, and easy accessibility to national markets.

The emergence of the Manufacturing Belt as the industrial heartland set the basic conditions for regional growth throughout the nation, particularly for the development of the "newer" regions. As its input requirements expanded, it reached into the outlying areas for its resources, stimulating their growth in ways dependent upon its resource demands and their endowment. The effect upon the outlying regions was to generate smaller clusters of industrialized growth to provide for the needs of their growing populations. And these, in turn, stimulated further clusters as manufacturing and service activities gained in volume and spread across the country. The rapid growth of the United States economy was accompanied, and to some extent achieved, by this process of industrial nucleation or clustering.

A major consequence of the process of expansion and regional differentiation has been the *specialization* of regional roles in the national economy. Within the Manufacturing Belt, where manufacturing specialization has been strong and continuous since 1870, the trend of manufacturing growth relative to that of the nation's has been westward to the Great Lakes area, while the shares of the New England and Middle Atlantic regions have declined. This is a natural consequence of a gradual spread of population westward. Large markets and production activities have followed this movement, and the superior resource endowment of the western end of the Manufacturing Belt has helped to tip the scales in its favor.

In resource activities, the great outlying regions (with the exception of the Far West) have maintained or increased their relative specialization while resource activity in the industrial heartland, in relative terms, has tended to decline. The Far West, especially California, is a unique case which, at least since the end of the nineteenth century, has followed neither heartland nor resource-hinterland patterns, but which might be described as a second-nucleation in the national economy. The development of California thus suggests some interesting questions concerning the possibility of "second growth" nucleations and the possibilities also of a gradual spreading out of relatively focused high-level development when advanced stages of national economic growth are reached.

The nature of these specializing processes has important implications for regional growth. In the resource regions, the working out of comparative advantage can result in a narrow and intensive specialization in a single resource subsector, in effect tying the future of the region to the vicissitudes of national demand for the products of that subsector. This will set ultimate limits to the region's growth rate: shifts in national demand patterns, the emergence of substitutes, depletion, technological advances, or the relative shifting of regional advantage may at any time choke off growth and leave behind enclaves of unemployed resources and economic stagnation. At its extreme, the Western experience of "boom town to ghost town" is a dramatic illustration, but almost as severe has been the history of the backland cotton-producing areas of the Southeast. These consequences are not confined to single-product specialization. Broader, sector-wide regional specialization may produce similar problems when the degree of specialization is great and when the products in the aggregate have a low income elasticity of demand. Typical of this kind of problem is the experience of some of the Plains states which have been increasing specialization in agriculture since 1910 at the same time that their relative contribution to the total national value of agricultural products has been declining.

On the other hand, the broad and diverse resource specialization involving products in growing demand may provide a continuing impetus to regional expansion, especially where there is some complementarity among the resource activities. The Southwest illustrates the advantages of such a condition. Here a flourishing chemical industry has emerged, based on rich endowments of petroleum, natural gas, sulfur, and salt. This is doubly fortunate, considering the high rate of growth of chemical industries in the national economy.

In short, then, the economic expansion of the resource-hinterlands has been closely associated historically with their resource endowments and the manner in which their endowments contributed to the evolution of favorable patterns of specialization or substantial levels of cumulative advantage.

Specialization within manufacturing is also a significant element in the growth patterns of regions. The economic expansion of the regions outside the Manufacturing Belt has been accompanied by some induced manufacturing growth which is largely centered on the processing of regional resource products. If manufacturing is classified into two classes — first stage resource users or "processing" industries, and later-stage or "fabricating" industries — and these are plotted by state economic areas (see Figure 4), it is clear that processing industries dominate throughout the resource-hinterlands, while fabricating industries dominate in the industrial heartland.[1] Thus the process of industrialization has not only defined the resource role of the "outlying" regions, but also sorted out the kinds of manufacturing activities between the industrial heartland and the "outlying" regions.

There has been another type of induced industrial growth, however. This relates to the role of region-serving industries in the regional growth process. These are generally market-oriented industries, producing products for a steadily increasing regional final demand. This kind of "filling in" growth has inevitably taken place at the expense of imports from other regions, so that one characteristic of regional growth has been the decline in relative export advantage of "older" regions which once provided goods for "newer" regions. This "filling in" process has played a large part in the economic growth of the Southeast and the West since 1870.

To sum up, while resource activities declined in relative importance in the national economy throughout the 1870-1950 period, the role they played historically defined the economic basis for succeeding stages of economic growth. In a very real sense the classical resource effects were playing themselves out, as over the past thirty to forty years the service sector moved into dominant position, and as technological and other changes (such as price changes which made recapture of waste products economical) brought about a long-range reduction in the proportion of raw materials to total output, thus weakening the linkage of economic activities to the resource inputs. The "market magnet" now operated as the dominant locational force in the economy.[2]

The Services Era and Amenity Resources

By mid-century, an additional resource effect was beginning to influence the regional distribution of economic activity. This was re-

[1]Industries classified as "processing" are those having a significant proportion of their labor force in sub-industry groups identified as first-stage resource users on the Census 3-digit basis. On this basis, the processing industries are: furniture and lumber and wood products; primary metal industries; food and kindred products; textile mill products; "other nondurable" goods. All other manufacturing industries have been classified as fabricating industries.

[2]Between 1870-74 and 1953-57, when real gross national product expanded 16 times, the output of all resource industries together rose less than 5 times. Resource industries output thus dropped from 46 per cent of GNP to about 14 per cent. Of these industries, agriculture, forestry, and fishing showed relative declines while mining rose from 2 per cent of GNP to 4.5 per cent in 1929 and then declined moderately to 3.5 per cent in 1953-57.

Figure 4
Type of Manufacturing Specialization, 1950, by State Economic Areas

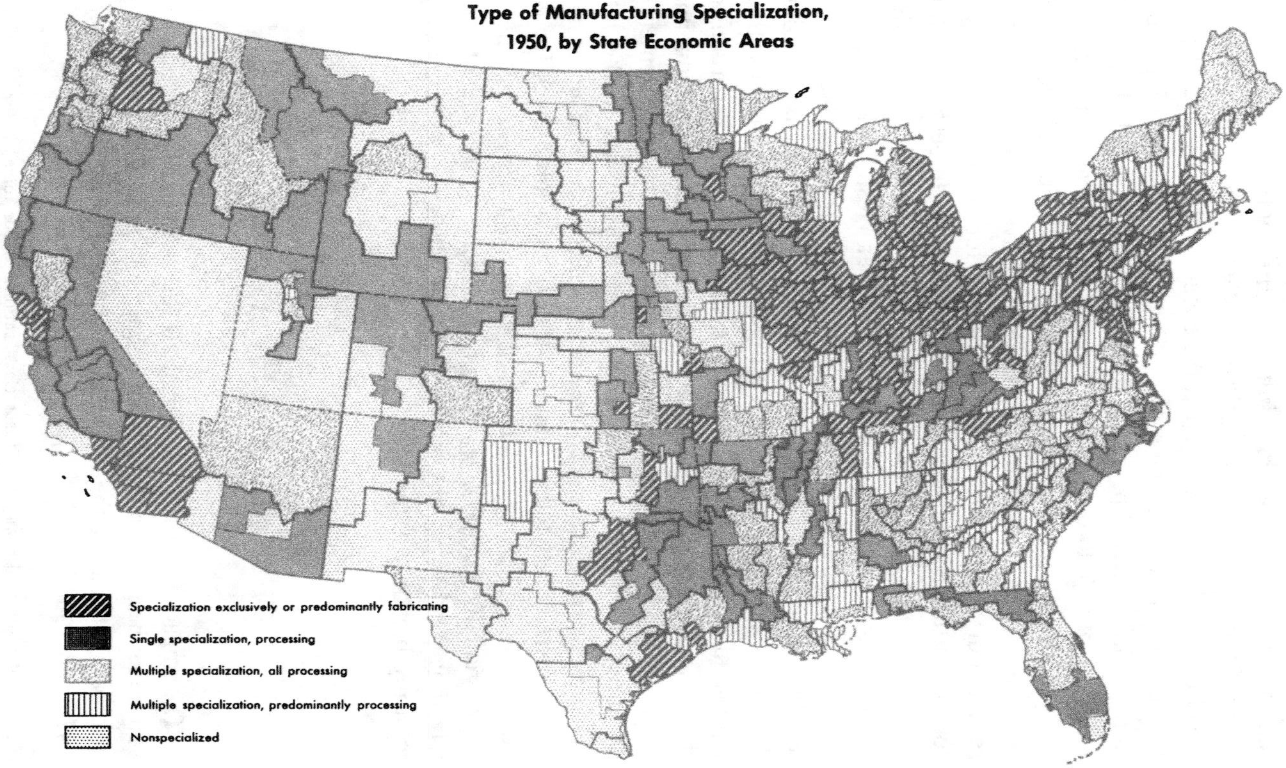

lated to the rapidly growing importance of "amenity resources" – that special juxtaposition of climate, land, coastline, and water offering conditions of living which influence directly the location of population (and, therefore, of markets), as well as of production. The effect of amenity resources upon the economy derives from the interplay of recent developments, two of which – the increasing proportions of older, retired people in the United States population and the tendency of foot-loose industries to settle in the amenity-rich areas – have already been mentioned. Rising per capita income has also been important. Increasing demand for travel and recreation has resulted in an increasing export market for regional amenity resources in the form of services to vacationers. Even before 1950, the great shift in population was toward areas that had these kinds of advantages: Florida, the Southwest, and Far West. Today the movement in those directions remains strong, although it is impossible to tell how much its effect upon specific regions can be attributed directly to this influence. Given a highly mobile population with rising incomes and retirement payments, however, it seems certain that the attraction of amenity resources will increase rather than diminish.

So, in the broad perspective of history, the changing content of resource endowment has had a succession of effects in the interregional distribution of economic activity. As "new" resources move to the forefront of the national economy, new advantages for economic growth are created for well endowed regions; and, in this interregionally competitive economy, as some gain from the new advantages other regions tend to lose their relative standing in the total production picture.

Changing Employment Patterns

The impact upon the regions of all the changing forces described above can best be summarized by recording, in Table 3, the changes in broad patterns of the labor force of the various regions between 1870 and 1960.[3]

[3]Because of substantial change in Census classifications, "labor force" is used here as the most accurate means of comparing increases in industrial activities over the ninety-year period (in spite of the 1940 change influencing the labor force figures). Labor force includes workers unemployed at the time of Census enumeration.

The nation's "primary" labor force – workers in farming, forestry, fishing, and mining – rose steeply between 1870 and 1910 and then declined as sharply, reaching a level in 1960 well below that of 1870. The manufacturing labor force doubled between 1870 and 1890, doubled again between 1890 and 1910, and despite a leveling off during the 1930's because of the great depression, continued to climb in succeeding twenty-year periods, though not so rapidly. The services labor force rose markedly throughout the whole period.

Primary Activities

The redistribution of primary activities across the nation, in terms of shares of the nation's resource activities, was considerably less between 1910 and 1960 than during the preceding forty years. The evolving pattern tells us something of how the regions reached their present resource relationships. Between 1910 and 1960 there was a decrease in the proportion of the total agricultural labor force located in the Southeast – from 44 per cent to 31 per cent – and a somewhat larger concentration in the entire greater West outside the Southwest, particularly in the Plains. The Plains states accounted for 15 per cent of the agricultural labor force in 1910 and 22 per cent in 1960. The major belts of farm staples largely remained unchanged except at their perimeters. Forestry and logging activities declined relatively in the New England, Middle Atlantic and Great Lakes regions, from 26 per cent in 1910 to 15 per cent in 1960. They also declined somewhat in the four regions of the greater West. The share of the Southwest meanwhile rose substantially from 35 per cent to 52 per cent – the only region to have increased its relative share. Mineral activities (including petroleum and natural gas extraction) experienced the greatest redistribution between 1910 and 1960. The share of the Northeast regions declined sharply, from 57 per cent of the total to 24 per cent. The Plains, Mountain, and Far West regions maintained their relative positions, while the Southeast almost doubled its share of mineral activities, from 17 per cent of the nation's mining labor force to 31 per cent, and the Southwest leaped from 4 per cent of the total to 26 per cent. Most of the redistribution in mineral activity came about through the change in the relative position of coal and oil products in the nation's fuel economy.

Table 3. **Labor Force in primary, manufacturing, and tertiary activities, and percentage changes by regions, 1870-1960**

Region	1870	1890	1910	1930* (1920 basis)	1930* (1940 basis)	1940	1950	1960**
LABOR FORCE (in thousands)								
Primary Activities								
United States	*6,684*	*9,865*	*13,597*	*11,707*	*11,590*	*9,860*	*8,185*	*4,960*
New England	363	360	311	241	236	180	152	93
Middle Atlantic	993	1,216	1,316	1,022	1,061	804	665	373
Great Lakes	1,567	1,988	2,046	1,621	1,607	1,391	1,167	733
Southeast	2,655	3,717	5,757	4,677	4,601	3,933	3,115	1,596
Plains	722	1,590	1,913	1,762	1,723	1,542	1,381	939
Southwest	202	522	1,415	1,352	1,335	1,118	850	576
Mountain	43	161	333	389	389	318	289	215
Far West	140	311	504	643	638	574	566	435
Manufacturing Industries								
United States	*2,643*	*5,526*	*10,657*	*14,111*	*10,481*	*10,426*	*14,399*	*17,307*
New England	572	960	1,430	1,479	1,099	1,158	1,381	1,470
Middle Atlantic	1,014	1,980	3,575	4,277	3,176	3,232	4,192	4,581
Great Lakes	538	1,173	2,409	3,611	2,682	2,909	4,167	4,655
Southeast	263	576	1,352	2,029	1,507	1,636	2,222	2,892
Plains	172	491	890	1,003	745	550	818	1,030
Southwest	19	72	292	583	433	275	472	714
Mountain	9	80	175	189	140	79	125	207
Far West	56	193	533	940	698	588	1,022	1,759
Tertiary Activities								
United States	*3,178*	*7,345*	*13,914*	*23,012*	*25,333*	*29,339*	*37,617*	*47,244*
New England	364	686	1,173	1,712	1,996	2,044	2,359	2,768
Middle Atlantic	1,149	2,328	4,102	6,674	7,386	8,242	9,265	10,763
Great Lakes	634	1,526	2,804	4,876	5,524	5,772	7,129	8,741
Southeast	590	1,185	2,244	3,555	3,853	5,056	7,147	9,632
Plains	262	906	1,647	2,287	2,437	2,790	3,352	3,950
Southwest	51	203	657	1,406	1,477	1,999	2,968	3,999
Mountain	18	157	345	467	484	634	918	1,213
Far West	110	355	942	2,034	2,176	2,802	4,480	6,179

*The Census Bureau occupational classifications were drastically revised in 1940, therefore two sets of 1930 data are shown, comparable to the earlier and following decades respectively. The percentage changes in the second half of the table compare the first set of 1930 data with the earlier years, and the second set with the later years.

**1960 Census data not adjusted to include 10-13 year-old employed persons.

Table 3. (cont.) **Labor Force in primary, manufacturing, and tertiary activities, and percentage changes by regions, 1870-1960**

Region	1870-90	1890-1910	1910-30 (1920 basis)	1930-50 (1940 basis)	1940-60
PERCENTAGE CHANGE IN LABOR FORCE					
Primary Activities					
United States	*47.6*	*37.8*	*— 13.9*	*— 29.4*	*— 49.7*
New England	— .8	— 13.5	— 22.5	— 35.6	— 48.3
Middle Atlantic	22.5	8.2	— 22.4	— 37.3	— 53.6
Great Lakes	26.9	2.9	— 20.8	— 27.4	— 47.3
Southeast	40.0	54.9	— 18.8	— 32.3	— 59.4
Plains	120.3	20.3	— 7.9	— 19.8	— 39.1
Southwest	158.5	171.2	— 4.5	— 36.3	— 48.5
Mountain	275.9	107.2	16.7	— 25.7	— 32.4
Far West	121.4	62.3	27.4	— 11.3	— 24.2
Manufacturing Industries					
United States	*109.0*	*92.9*	*32.4*	*37.4*	*66.0*
New England	67.8	48.9	3.4	25.7	26.9
Middle Atlantic	95.4	80.5	19.6	32.0	41.7
Great Lakes	118.0	105.4	49.9	64.4	60.0
Southeast	119.1	134.9	50.0	47.4	76.8
Plains	184.7	81.3	12.7	9.8	87.3
Southwest	280.3	303.4	99.6	9.0	159.6
Mountain	760.0	119.6	8.2	— 10.7	162.0
Far West	246.7	175.5	76.4	46.4	199.1
Tertiary Activities					
United States	*131.1*	*89.4*	*65.4*	*48.5*	*61.0*
New England	88.5	71.0	46.0	18.2	35.4
Middle Atlantic	102.7	76.2	62.7	25.4	30.6
Great Lakes	140.6	83.8	73.9	29.1	51.4
Southeast	101.0	89.4	58.4	85.5	90.5
Plains	245.7	81.7	38.8	37.5	41.6
Southwest	296.2	223.9	114.1	100.9	100.0
Mountain	752.7	119.5	35.4	89.7	91.3
Far West	221.7	165.5	116.0	105.9	120.5

Manufacturing Activities

The pattern of regional manufacturing development shown by the data in Table 3 demonstrates the interregional leveling process that has been under way as the nation's economy has matured. Thus, during the past two decades the Southwest, Mountain, and Far West regions increased their manufacturing labor force much more rapidly than the other sections of the country, ranging from an increase of 160 per cent in the Southwest to almost 200 per cent in the Far West.

Looked at in terms of each region's share of the nation's manufacturing development, however, the enduring strength of the urban-industrial Northeast is evident. After ninety years of continuing industrial transformation, nearly two-thirds of the nation's manufacturing labor force was *still* located in the Northeastern industrial belt in 1960.

Table 4 expresses this development through 1950 in figures for "value added by manufacture," which, by eliminating the cost of material inputs indicates how much of the final value of a product is attributable to the manufacturing industry involved.

Table 4. Regional distribution of U.S. value added by manufacture, 1870, 1890, 1910, 1930, and 1950

Region	1870	1890	1910	1930	1950
United States*	$1,577 100%	$3,454 100%	$8,189 100%	$30,694 100%	$74,354 100%
New England	23.95	17.48	14.32	10.35	9.16
Middle Atlantic	42.16	40.05	36.90	33.75	29.87
Great Lakes	18.07	24.35	25.59	31.63	31.57
Southeast	6.23	6.83	10.04	9.86	12.49
Plains	6.68	7.00	6.42	5.74	5.54
Southwest	.31	.68	1.49	2.00	3.00
Mountain	.24	.68	1.21	.95	.88
Far West	2.36	2.93	4.03	5.72	7.49

*U. S. total value added in millions of current dollars.

In general, changes in each region's share of total value added by manufacture parallel changes in its share of total manufacturing labor force. However, in the recent years two regions have deviated somewhat from the close parallel existing in the other six: the Southeast had a larger share of manufacturing labor force than of value-added (15 per cent as against 12.5 per cent in 1950), while the Great Lakes region had a larger share of value-added than of manufacturing labor force (32 per cent as against 29 per cent). It is significant perhaps that before 1930 the Middle Atlantic region had a larger share of value-added than of manufacturing labor force (37 per cent as against 34 per cent in 1910). The implication of these developments, therefore, is that the Great Lakes region has become the nation's most productive manufacturing region (in terms of value-added per worker) and that the Southeast is relatively the least productive in this sense. This is due in large part to the fact that capital invested per worker (and wage levels) is higher in the Great Lakes than in the Southeast, but other factors have contributed as well. However, these comparisons are relative; there has been a marked increase in labor productivity in manufacturing throughout the entire country.

Service Activities

The tertiary or service sector of the economy has often been regarded as itself a key measure of economic development and material progress. As technical and organizational advances in the primary (resource) and secondary (manufacturing) sectors have augmented labor productivity, a growing proportion of the labor force has been freed from resource extraction and manufactures to engage in so-called services to business and consumers – that is, in transportation and communications, wholesale and retail trade, finance, government, recreation, the professions, and other services to individuals.

While resource labor force, the bulk of which is still agricultural, declined absolutely and relatively after 1910 and manufacturing declined relatively after 1920, the labor force in services has grown steadily so that in 1960 it constituted two-thirds of the total labor force.

Because the service sector of the economy is commonly defined as "all other activities" – that is, as the total labor force less the workers engaged in primary and secondary activities – so many different types of activities are involved that generalizations as to their character and significance are subject to a considerable degree of error. It is well to bear this in mind when looking at the services activities of the regions in Table 5. These are expressed in terms of labor force distribution (i.e., regional shares of the nation's labor force engaged in service activities) between 1870 and 1950.

Table 5. Regional distribution of services labor force, 1870, 1890, 1910, 1930, and 1950

Region	1870	1890	1910	1930	1950
United States	3,178,287 100%	7,345,373 100%	13,913,976 100%	23,012,448 100%	37,617,484 100%
New England	11.45	9.34	8.43	7.44	6.27
Middle Atlantic	36.14	31.69	29.48	29.00	24.63
Great Lakes	19.95	20.77	20.15	21.19	18.95
Southeast	18.55	16.13	16.13	15.45	19.00
Plains	8.25	12.34	11.84	9.94	8.91
Southwest	1.61	2.76	4.72	6.11	7.89
Mountain	.58	2.14	2.48	2.03	2.44
Far West	3.47	4.83	6.77	8.84	11.91

In general, it is becoming evident that while regional specialization is still the dominant feature of the American economic landscape, the various regions of the country are developing broader economic bases with not-insignificant components of all the major industries. In other words, regions tend over time to become more alike – although the process is almost glacial in its over-all impact. It is important to identify the direction of change; it is equally important to note the pace.

4. Growth of the States in Recent Years: 1939-1958

Against the background of century-long economic changes among the great regions of the country, the growth of the various states in recent decades can be placed in proper perspective.[1] The emphasis throughout this chapter is on the states' differing rates of growth when these are compared with the nation's average rate of growth. The aim is to identify those sections of the country that have grown more than the national average, and those that have grown less.

As people and industry moved into areas which, prior to the economic build-up associated with World War II, had experienced only moderate development – Texas and Florida, for example – the spurt of growth in population and total and per capita income in these areas tends to dominate the regional scene. Yet it is equally true that the established industrialized areas, such as those located in the Middle Atlantic and Great Lakes regions, steadily increased their contributions to national economic growth. The fact that, in both volume and welfare measures, the growth of these areas started from a higher level in 1939 than the more recently industrialized areas results in smaller percentage increases when compared with the economic growth of the nation as a whole.

This relationship of the growth rate of a state or region to that of the nation over the recent twenty years helps to point up the gradual

[1]To provide a time period similar to that used when changes in employment patterns are examined in later chapters, the main focus here is on the years from 1939 to 1958. These are the years for which the Census of Manufactures provides the necessary detail. The first and last years of this period have somewhat comparable business-cycle [particularly unemployment] characteristics. Actually, however, no years during the twentieth century chosen for growth comparisons are entirely removed from "unusual" factors associated with war and depression. Because of this, in some cases figures for earlier or later years are used as a check upon the validity of the conclusions drawn from the 1939-58 data (as well as for the additional information they contribute).

Table 6. Changes in population, total personal income, and per capita income among states, 1939-1958

	ABSOLUTE CHANGES 1939-58					PERCENTAGE CHANGES 1939-58				
		Total personal income		Per capita income			Total personal income		Per capita income	
	Population (thousands)	Current dollars (millions)	1958 dollars (millions)	Current dollars	1958 dollars	Population	Current dollars	1958 dollars	Current dollars	1958 dollars
Cont. U.S.	*42,380*	*284,789*	*206,289*	*1,513*	*913*	*32.4*	*391*	*136.4*	*272*	*79.0*
*Group I**										
Fla.	2,606	7,475	6,513	1,396	872	141.9	838	351.3	287	86.3
Ariz.	656	1,971	1,722	1,416	901	135.5	853	358.8	297	90.9
N. M.	319	1,370	1,171	1,396	1,016	61.0	745	305.7	397	138.9
Utah	322	1,265	994	1,305	806	59.3	504	190.4	282	84.0
Colo.	591	2,930	2,306	1,518	961	52.8	507	191.8	294	89.6
Texas	3,017	14,529	11,724	1,438	997	47.4	559	216.9	352	117.2
Va.	1,265	5,533	4,317	1,326	871	47.4	491	184.2	314	99.2
Ind.	1,178	7,355	5,448	1,487	927	34.6	416	148.3	287	85.9
La.	776	4,099	3,199	1,180	795	33.2	491	184.5	331	107.1
Group II										
No. Car.	1,035	5,207	4,008	1,090	749	29.5	469	173.5	345	114.0
So. Car.	532	2,413	1,862	974	679	28.4	472	175.3	357	119.7
Idaho	141	901	657	1,289	821	27.1	399	139.8	297	91.0
Ga.	698	4,705	3,662	1,161	826	22.4	487	182.2	375	128.2
Tenn.	595	4,142	3,186	1,133	801	20.7	467	173.0	368	125.1
Kan.	292	3,520	2,771	1,603	1,193	16.0	507	192.0	422	151.0
Ala.	397	3,675	2,915	1,105	835	14.1	522	199.1	442	160.7
Neb.	139	2,238	1,676	1,584	1,158	10.5	430	154.8	401	141.0
Ky.	255	3,481	2,558	1,153	826	9.0	407	143.9	381	131.1
So. Dak.	54	913	677	1,308	941	8.4	417	148.8	385	133.1
No. Dak.	16	861	643	1,363	1,024	.9	426	153.1	434	156.9
Miss.	18	1,854	1,375	865	644	.8	418	149.0	422	151.1

Group III										
Wis.	817	6,033	4,290	1,476	918	26.2	374	127.8	285	85.4
Mont.	133	1,048	731	1,494	922	24.0	356	119.6	282	83.7
Minn.	604	5,054	3,509	1,425	867	21.8	353	117.9	276	80.7
Mo.	488	6,730	4,665	1,515	969	12.9	352	117.2	299	92.1
Iowa	302	4,073	2,797	1,449	943	12.0	344	113.7	309	96.7
W. Va.	101	2,237	1,457	1,189	771	5.4	309	96.9	307	95.9
Okla.	—48	3,149	2,280	1,383	1,011	—2.1	391	136.2	401	140.9
Ark.	—182	1,681	1,173	958	697	—9.3	357	119.8	396	138.5
Group IV										
Nev.	160	595	498	1,734	827	149.5	661	266.3	206	47.3
Calif.	7,552	31,874	26,202	1,718	882	111.3	606	239.7	222	54.7
Del.	191	1,007	747	1,940	952	72.6	418	149.1	212	50.0
Md.	1,163	5,475	4,195	1,587	874	64.9	462	170.1	240	63.6
Ore.	692	2,899	2,220	1,435	807	64.0	461	169.7	247	66.7
Wash.	1,054	4,919	3,777	1,556	890	61.5	465	171.7	252	69.4
Mich.	2,710	13,366	9,897	1,542	869	52.6	416	148.1	247	67.0
Group V										
N. J.	1,620	11,342	7,997	1,745	935	39.2	366	124.1	232	59.9
Conn.	620	5,091	3,564	1,882	982	36.6	360	121.1	226	56.6
Ohio	2,459	16,262	11,660	1,587	919	35.7	381	131.5	256	71.4
Group VI										
Wyo.	72	531	375	1,501	870	29.0	366	124.6	257	71.5
D. C.	167	1,391	598	1,733	528	25.4	189	39.1	155	22.7
Ill.	11,999	18,664	12,658	1,796	1,035	25.3	335	109.4	255	70.6
R. I.	174	1,226	686	1,332	563	24.8	245	66.0	187	38.0
N. Y.	2,706	31,005	18,972	1,761	871	20.0	278	81.8	213	50.8
N. H.	94	831	535	1,327	724	19.2	303	93.9	237	62.3
Me.	106	1,225	775	1,214	682	12.5	294	89.4	246	66.6
Pa.	1,200	17,656	11,254	1,543	897	12.1	298	91.2	258	72.0
Mass.	515	8,515	5,103	1,608	824	11.8	269	77.6	221	54.5
Vt.	14	473	287	1,191	673	3.9	275	80.2	248	67.5

* Group I. Population, total income, and per capita income — all above-average increases.
Group II. Population — below-average; total and per capita income — both above-average increases.
Group III. Population and total income — below-average increases; per capita income — above-average increases.
Group IV. Population and total income — above-average increases; per capita income — below-average increases.
Group V. Population — above-average increases; total and per capita income — below-average increases.
Group VI. Population, total income, and per capita income — all below-average increases.

convergence of per capita income in different parts of the country toward the national average. In 1939, for example, regional averages of per capita income ranged from a high of 133 per cent of the national average (in the Middle Atlantic) to a low of 57 per cent (in the Southeast). In 1958, the highest regional income was 118 per cent of the national average and the lowest 72 per cent.

It goes without saying that there are still wide disparities in *absolute* per capita income among the states. Table 6 makes it abundantly clear that there are significant differences between absolute increases and percentage increases, whether in population, total income, or per capita income. A state like Arizona, for example, can show a 135.5 per cent population increase between 1939 and 1958 with a gain in total numbers of 656,000, while Nevada can show a gain of 149.5 per cent with an increase of 160,000 people. Conversely, a state like New York which gained 2,706,000 people during the same period (the fourth largest increase in the country) shows a percentage gain that is below the national average (20 per cent versus a national average of 32.4 per cent).

In absolute terms, the income gains among the states over the period 1939-58 have been within a relatively narrow range. The most significant divergence between the absolute and relative figures is found in the case of the Southeastern states, which on the whole had the largest percentage increases but well below average absolute increase. This has been the situation for quite some period of time. The Southeast as a whole has had *percentage* increases in per capita income greater than the national average for every decade except one since 1900; yet, during the same period, there has been only one decade in which *absolute* increments in per capita income have exceeded the national average in any Southeastern state except Florida. Thus, despite its percentage gains in relation to the national average, the Southeast has lagged behind other regions in terms of improving its absolute levels of per capita income.

Table 6 also shows how different can be the relationship between increases in volume (population and total personal income) and increases in welfare (per capita income) among the states. Few states that experienced above-average increases in per capita income had commensurate increases in population; most, in fact, improved their welfare with a relative loss, and sometimes an absolute loss, of population (see Groups II and III). Included among these are most of the Southeastern states and some of the Plains states.

The rapid volume growth of the Far West is one of the features reflected in Group IV. In all four states population and total income have climbed steadily beyond the average growth for the nation. In recent years, however, per capita income in these states has not grown as fast as the national average – a natural effect, no doubt, of a large influx of families earning low wages seeking better levels of living in a fast-growing area.

New Jersey, Connecticut, and Ohio – the Group V states – had below-average increases in both total and per capita income, while heavy urbanization and, in New Jersey and Connecticut, suburbanization from New York City, account for the above-average increases in population.

With the exception of Connecticut, all the New England states, as well as the highly industrialized states of New York, Pennsylvania, and Illinois, have increased at a rate below the national average in population and total and per capita income (see Group VI). Here we have the effects of a slowing down in relative rates of growth of the more "mature" sections of the country.

A Special Measure of Differential Growth

No fully satisfactory way of combining percentage and absolute changes has yet been devised to measure differential economic growth. However, by using a "shift" method of presenting data, it is possible to see the relative size of the gains or losses among the areas being compared. This method helps to avoid the distortion apparent when percentage figures alone are used – as, for example, when California's increase in population of over 7 million during 1939-58 is shown as a 111 per cent increase and Nevada's growth in population of 160,000 is shown as a 150 per cent gain. The "shift" measure can be applied to any type of area, whether multi-state, state, or substate, and whether the variable be population, income, or employment. It is used for analysis throughout this study.

First, it is necessary to explain what is being measured when "shifts" are used to express a change in a state's relative standing. Growth in population will be taken as an example. Between 1939 and 1958 the population of the United States increased by 42 million. This represents a percentage increase over 1939 of 32.4 per cent.

Table 7. Summary of net shifts in U.S. population and examples of state shifts, 1939-1958

	Continental United States		States with upward shifts (19)		States with downward shifts (29 and D.C.)	
	Per cent	Population	Per cent	Population	Per cent	Population
1. 1939		130,880,000		48,880,000		82,000,000
2. 1958		173,260,000		77,835,000		95,425,000
3. Actual increase	32.38	42,380,00		28,951,000		13,425,000
4. *(Expected growth of the states)*			(32.38)	(15,825,000)	(32.38)	(26,551,000)
5. Total net shifts (the difference between actual and expected growth)				+13,126,000		—13,126,000

Examples of State Shifts

	California	New York	Kansas
6. 1939	6,785,000	13,523,000	1,824,000
7. 1958	14,337,000	16,229,000	2,116,000
8. Actual increase	7,552,000	2,706,000	292,000
9. *(Expected increase)*	*(2,197,000)*	*(4,379,000)*	*(591,000)*
10. State's upward or downward shift (difference between actual and expected growth)	+5,355,000	—1,673,000	—299,000
11. State's shift as percentage of total net shift (Line 10 as % of line 5)[a]	40.8%	12.7%	2.3%

[a] It should be noted that the totals of the upward and the downward shifts for the nation are each 13,126,000 (100 per cent), and that the shift for each state indicates that state's share of all state upward shifts or of all state downward shifts, as the case may be. These percentage figures are the ones shown on the shift charts; for example, note California's population growth of 40.8 per cent in Figure 5, indicating that California had 40.8 per cent of the total upward shifts.

Naturally, not all of the states grew at this national average rate. Some of them grew at higher rates than the nation's 32.4 per cent — higher, that is, than what might be termed their *expected* rate of growth — and some at lesser rates. When all the states' deviations from *expected* growth are added together they amount to no more than 13,126,000; but it is the distribution of these 13 million among the states that provides the key to measuring changes in the states' relative standings as related to the growth of the nation as a whole. The national shift pattern, summarized in Table 7, shows how *expected* growth compares with actual growth and results in the total net shift figure for the nation.

What happens when we apply this method of computing relative standing to specific states? As can be seen from the tabulation, California's *expected* population growth between 1939 and 1958 – i.e., the increase that would have taken place if it had grown at the national rate of 32.4 per cent over the period – was 2.2 million people. Its *actual* growth, however, was 7.5 million. California's "extra" growth, or "net upward shift" in population, is therefore 5.3 million. When this figure is compared to all the extra growth, it turns out to be 40.8 per cent *of all the upward shifts* experienced across the nation. New York, on the other hand, is an illustration of a state showing an *actual* increase in population, but a downward shift because the rate of increase experienced was lower than the national 32.4 per cent rate of increase.

Applying the Shift Technique

The process of "filling in" the more sparsely populated parts of the country, demonstrated by the net population shifts among the states shown in Figure 5, has been going on for longer than the period 1939-58 of course. But, the trends are similar whether one looks back over two decades or half a century.

Whether the period examined is 1939-58 or 1910-57 (the difference in the terminal date is to avoid tieing both comparisons to the same year), four states lead in relative growth of population: California's share of all net upward shifts for the shorter period, 40.8 per cent, compares with 43.11 per cent for the period 1910-1957; Michigan, with 7.9 per cent of the net upward shifts between 1939 and 1958 had 11.77 per cent of the total over the longer period. With Florida and Texas, these four are clearly the outstanding population-growth states of the twentieth century.

Using the same process of shift analysis as has been applied to population, these same states, with the exception of Michigan, also show the greatest relative increases in total personal income over the 1939-58 period (Figure 6). At the other end of the scale, the four highly industrialized states of Illinois, Pennsylvania, New York, and

Figure 5
Percentage Distribution of Net Shifts
in Total Population, 1939-1958

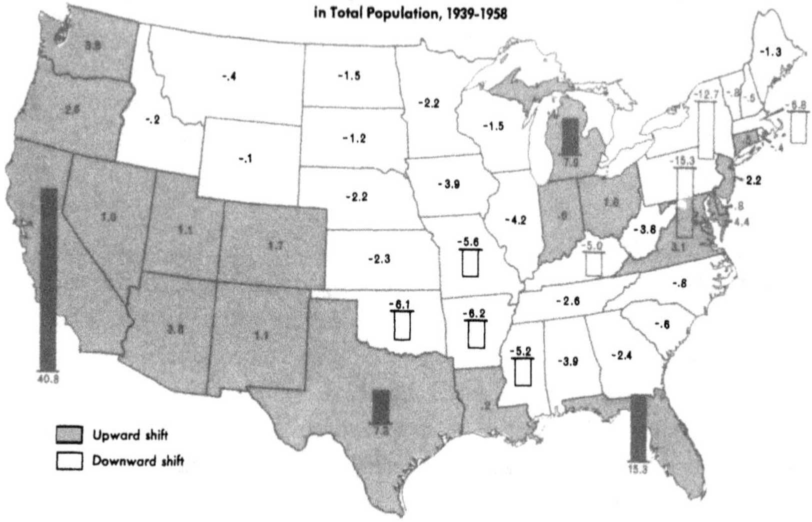

Figure 6
Percentage Distribution of Net Shifts
in Total Personal Income, 1939-1958

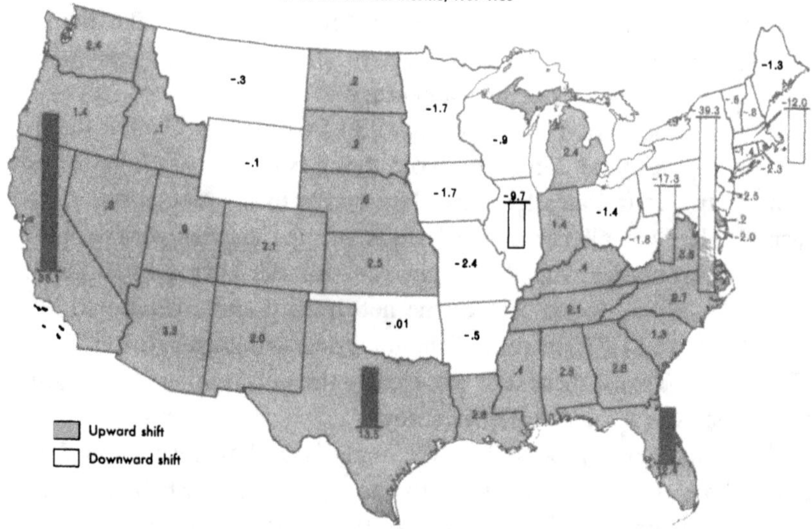

Massachusetts accounted for 78 per cent of the net *downward* shift in total income, despite their high rank when income is measured in absolute terms.

The main divergences between changes in relative population standing and relative total income standing occurred in the Southeast, where the states improved their relative standing on total income between 1939 and 1958 but had downward shifts in population. There was some divergence between population and total income changes in the Plains states also; all of these states had net downward shifts in population, but a number of them (the Dakotas, Kansas, and Nebraska) improved their income standing, mainly as a result of World War II demands for increased agricultural production and for industries and services located there, far from the coasts. For the postwar years, the Plains states show no gain in relative standing on total income; and this is true also for most of the states in the Deep South; Georgia and South Carolina are exceptions. On the other hand, since World War II, the Middle Atlantic seaboard states show a gain in relative income standing.

The World War II period clearly is atypical of the longer-run trends. But if total income for all the states during the postwar years were to be compared with that for a longer period of time – one reaching back to 1920 for instance – the pattern of differential gains among the states since the war would be found to correspond quite closely with that for the longer period.

5. Recent Shifts in Employment Among the States: 1939-1958

A detailed analysis of the change in the distribution of employment among the states between 1939 and 1958 reveals important characteristics of the regional distribution of economic activity. Employment is used here as the measure of the growth in the volume of economic activity.

The period examined is 1939-1958, since the most reliable data on the distribution of total employment is available for that period. The same period is used for mining and manufacturing when their industry components are analyzed for their contributions to the change in employment distribution by states.[1] Analysis was made of preliminary Census data for 1-digit industry categories published in 1960.

National Shift in Job Distribution

The shift method of analysis, introduced in Chapter 4 to show relative population growth among the states, is used here also to analyze employment shifts. The merit of this method lies in its focus on the differential rates of regional change, rather than on total changes, which tend to hide the differential through sheer weight of numbers. Table 8 presents the state-by-state data for 1939 employment, 1958 employment, the absolute change, the net shift, and each state's net shift as a percentage of the national net shift. The net shift pattern may be seen graphically in the map presented in Figure 7. Here again, the percentage figures on this map represent percentages of the national shift and do not refer to a percentage increase or decrease in employment in a particular state.

[1]Agricultural activities, for which the measure of "value of agricultural products" rather than "employment" is used in detailed analysis, are examined for the years 1940-54.

Table 8. Total employment, absolute change, and net shift, 1939-1958

	Total Employment 1939	Total Employment 1958	Absolute Change	"Expected" Change	Net Shift	Percentage Shift
	(1)	(2)	(3)	(4)	(5)	(6)
United States	*40,908,238*	*58,274,086*	*17,365,848*	*17,365,846*	*± 3,887,730*	*± 100.00*
New England						
Maine	269,828	325,748	55,920	114,544	— 58,624	— 1.51
New Hampshire	161,042	196,499	35,458	68,364	— 32,906	— .85
Vermont	112,743	129,071	16,328	47,860	— 31,532	— .81
Massachusetts	1,380,159	1,836,843	456,684	585,888	— 129,204	— 3.32
Rhode Island	238,595	276,116	37,521	101,285	— 63,764	— 1.64
Connecticut	604,938	900,622	295,684	256,801	+ 38,883	+ 1.00
Middle Atlantic						
New York	4,355,449	6,255,141	1,899,692	1,848,920	+ 50,772	+ 1.31
New Jersey	1,250,876	1,977,941	727,065	531,006	+ 196,059	+ 5.04
Pennsylvania	2,958,315	3,828,490	870,175	1,255,826	— 385,651	— 9.92
Delaware	84,819	162.591	77,772	36,006	+ 41,766	+ 1.07
Maryland & District of Columbia	887,163	1,414,264	527,101	376,607	+ 150,494	+ 3.87
Great Lakes						
Ohio	2,106,679	3,270,199	1,163,520	894,301	+ 269,219	+ 6.92
Indiana	1,068,169	1,567,103	498,934	453,446	+ 45,488	+ 1.17
Illinois	2,518,204	3,639,796	1,121,592	1,068,996	+ 52,596	+ 1.35
Michigan	1,634,953	2,421,093	786,140	694,049	+ 92,091	+ 2.37
Wisconsin	1,016,809	1,435,970	419,161	431,643	— 12,482	— .32

Southeast						
Virginia	815,553	1,171,794	356,241	346,208	+ 10,033	+ .26
West Virginia	514,851	535,665	20,814	218,558	— 197,744	— 5.09
North Carolina	1,164,638	1,523,397	358,759	494,397	— 135,638	— 3.49
South Carolina	679,221	731,278	52,057	288,334	— 236,277	— 6.08
Georgia	1,015,012	1,158,668	143,656	430,880	— 287,224	— 7.39
Florida	503,100	1,261,022	757,922	213,570	+ 544,352	+ 14.00
Kentucky	720,645	868,396	147,751	305,919	— 158,168	— 4.07
Tennessee	845,078	1,091,098	246,020	358,742	— 112,722	— 2.90
Alabama	852,549	874,370	21,821	361,913	— 340,092	— 8.75
Mississippi	787,145	644,552	— 142,593	334,149	— 476,742	— 12.26
Arkansas	630,568	564,253	— 66,315	267,681	— 333,996	— 8.59
Louisiana	717,341	909,105	191,764	304,516	— 112,752	— 2.90
Plains						
Minnesota	897,538	1,173,529	275,991	381,011	— 105,020	— 2.70
Iowa	769,712	939,445	169,733	326,748	— 157,015	— 4.04
Missouri	1,184,681	1,578,992	394,311	502,906	— 108,595	— 2.79
North Dakota	230,527	219,203	— 11,324	97,860	— 109,184	— 2.81
South Dakota	200,879	229,953	29,074	85,275	— 56,201	— 1.45
Nebraska	400,145	507,678	107,533	169,864	— 62,331	— 1.60
Kansas	500,880	708,371	207,491	212,627	— 5,136	— .13
Southwest						
Oklahoma	583,556	728,800	145,244	247,724	— 102,480	— 2.64
Texas	1,971,998	2,854,638	882,641	837,128	+ 45,513	+ 1.17
New Mexico	143,848	273,897	130,049	61,065	+ 68,984	+ 1.77
Arizona	140,440	332,293	191,853	59,618	+ 132,235	+ 3.40
Mountain						
Montana	188,838	214,827	25,989	80,163	— 54,174	— 1.39
Idaho	164,624	222,379	57,755	69,884	— 12,129	— .31
Wyoming	82,066	107,109	25,043	34,838	— 9,795	— .25
Colorado	326,752	535,242	208,490	138,709	+ 69,781	+ 1.79
Utah	149,176	275,554	126,378	63,326	+ 63,052	+ 1.62
Far West						
Washington	565,090	898,322	333,232	239,885	+ 93,347	+ 2.40
Oregon	365,178	569,156	203,978	155,021	+ 48,957	+ 1.26
California	2,106,122	4,841,968	2,735,846	894,064	+ 1,841,782	+ 47.37
Nevada	41,746	91,945	50,199	17,721	+ 32,478	+ .84

Figure 7
Percentage Distribution of Net Shifts
in Total Employment, 1939-1958

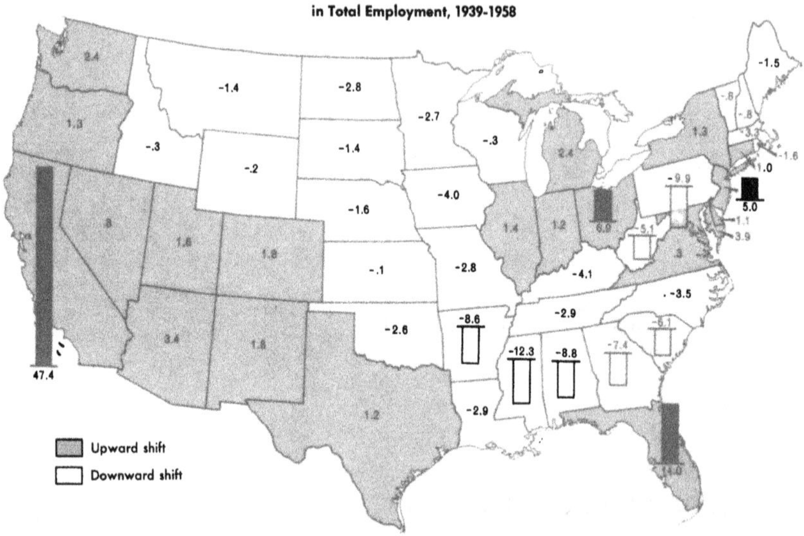

The total reported increase in jobs between 1939 and 1958, was 17,365,848, but the total shift was only 3,887,730 – that is, the latter number was distributed by states differently from the 1939 distribution pattern. California, for example, had 2,735,846 new jobs, of which 1,841,782 represented a positive shift, or an increase over the state's proportion of total jobs in 1939. This was 47.4 per cent of the total positive national shift of jobs.

The close tie between employment and population is apparent when one compares the job shift for each state in Figure 7 with the population shift in Figure 5. With the exception of only three states, the relative shifts in both measures between 1939 and 1958 take the same direction. Louisiana shows a downward shift in employment compared with an upward shift in population. Illinois and New York, on the other hand, show an upward shift in employment and a downward shift (but not an actual decline) in population.

Some Significant Conclusions

Turning to major employment categories, the same shift analysis was applied to each of the Census 1-digit employment sectors, such

Table 9. Relative importance of employment shifts within the major employment sectors, 1939-1958

1-Digit employment sectors	Employment				Absolute change 1939-58	Percentage increase (Col. 5 as per cent of Col. 1)	Total net shift 1939-58	Net shift as per cent of:	
	1939	Per cent	1958	Per cent				Absolute change	1939 employment
	(1)	(2)	(3)	(4)	(5)	(6)	(7)	(8)	(9)
Total employment	40,908,238	100.0	58,274,086	100.0	17,365,848	42.5	± 3,887,730	± 22.4	± 9.5
Construction	1,177,000	2.9	2,761,300	4.7	1,584,300	134.6	± 279,887	± 17.7	± 23.8
Government	3,987,100	9.8	7,920,000	13.6	3,932,900	98.6	± 781,049	± 19.9	± 19.6
Service and miscellaneous	3,339,700	8.2	6,206,800	10.6	2,867,100	85.8	± 349,409	± 12.2	± 10.5
Finance, insurance and real estate	1,364,700	3.3	2,397,400	4.1	1,032,700	75.7	± 301,535	± 29.2	± 22.1
Wholesale trade	1,605,347	3.9	2,788,138	4.8	1,182,791	73.7	± 229,969	± 19.4	± 14.3
Manufacturing	9,622,923	23.5	16,046,945	27.5	6,424,022	66.8	± 1,335,493	± 20.8	± 13.9
Retail trade	4,821,806	11.8	7,898,409	13.6	3,076,603	63.8	± 516,665	± 16.8	± 10.7
Transportation and public utilities	2,912,000	7.1	3,995,100	6.9	1,083,100	37.2	± 266,762	± 24.6	± 9.2
Mining	827,410	2.0	734,994	1.3	— 92,416	— 11.2	± 196,847	± 213.0	± 23.8
Agriculture	11,250,252	27.5	7,525,000	12.9	— 3,725,252	— 33.1	± 843,369	± 22.6	± 7.5

as construction, government, agriculture, and mining. The summary of the shifts is presented in Table 9. Several interesting conclusions are apparent from these data and some additional conclusions have been derived by further analysis.

The first conclusion is the large degree of stability in the growth pattern. Most of the growth during these two decades was distributed in accordance with the pattern of job distribution in 1939. The increase in jobs was 42.5 per cent, and over 77 per cent of this increase was in accordance with the existing distribution of total jobs, while less than 23 per cent represented a shift of location of job totals. If comparison is made with the total number of jobs in 1939, the number of jobs which represented a shift was actually only 9.5 per cent of this total, and only 6.7 per cent of the total number in 1958. The distribution of jobs at any given time appears to have a strong influence on the distribution of jobs in the limited future, that is, within one or two decades.

The second observation is the difference in growth patterns and in shift patterns for different major employment sectors. Construction, for example, increased 135 per cent while agriculture decreased by 33 per cent. The average increase for all employment was 42.5 per cent, but the dispersion around this average was quite wide. When the shift in employment among the states is compared with the absolute change in employment in a given industry, however, it appears that the percentage differences are smaller. The net shift as a per cent of absolute change for all employment was 22.4 per cent; and, omitting mining, the range of shift percentage for each industry is from 12.2 per cent for services to 29.2 per cent for finance, insurance, and real estate. In other words, the shift pattern for most industries was quite comparable to the average shift pattern for all employment. Since the rates of growth for the various employment categories varied widely, however, the net shift as a per cent of 1939 employment shows a slightly different pattern.

A further analysis of the data was made by making a correlation of each state's share of the employment in basic industry categories with each state's share of population in a given year, 1954. Correlation was based on the rank of each state in population and in each of the employment categories. The results are presented in Table 10. For total employment the rank correlation is .991. A very high correlation is achieved for employment in retail trade, service and miscellaneous, wholesale trade, and government. A high correlation is found for construction, for transportation and public utilities, and for finance, insurance, and real estate. There is a modest correlation for manufacturing employment; a low correlation for agricultural employment; and a very low correlation for mining employment.

Table 10. Rank correlations of each state's share of employment in selected industries with each state's share of population, 1954

Total employment .991			
Retail trade employment	.979	Transportation and public utility employment	.957
Service and miscellaneous employment	.972	Finance, insurance and real estate employment	.957
Wholesale trade employment	.970	Manufacturing employment	.936
Government employment	.970	Agricultural employment	.649
Construction employment	.960	Mining employment	.406

This finding is not surprising. The three categories least tied to population – mining, agriculture, and manufacturing – are those most devoted to serving national and international markets. The other categories are primarily devoted to employment serving local and, in some cases, regional markets. Distribution of employment serving the local market naturally is highly correlated with the distribution of population itself. In state-by-state aggregates the distribution of population and such employment would be quite similar.

The three categories least tied to population also happen to be the categories with the major share of the total job shifts during the 1939-1958 period. Agriculture, mining, and manufacturing together accounted for 61 per cent of the total job shift among the states. Total employment in these three categories in 1939 amounted to only 53 per cent of the total jobs, and in 1958 the total of these three categories was only 42 per cent of the total number of jobs. Shifts in these three categories have been a major factor in influencing the total number of job shifts, although not the only factors. Because of their importance, a separate chapter is devoted to each of these categories.

Other factors which may influence the relation of population to employment include the attraction of "amenity" areas for many persons for whom employment opportunity is not a prerequisite of residence, and the lag in an area's population adjustment to changes in economic opportunity. Statistical measurement may also be influenced by biased reporting of original data (to which agricultural areas in particular are susceptible).

Composition Effect and Local-Factor Effect

The relation between the rate of growth of an industry and its shift in location among the various states has been measured by a new statistical technique first introduced in the major volume from which this summary is largely drawn. This technique is based on the fact that when an industry is growing nationally because of increasing demand for its products, areas in which the nationally growing industry is located will grow because of this advantage. Conversely, regions containing slow-growth or declining industries will suffer as a consequence. This, for convenience, may be termed the *composition* or *industry-mix* effect.

Thus, those regions that tend to specialize in the slow-growth sectors – particularly of agriculture and mining – will show net downward composition shifts in total employment, while those that tend to specialize in the rapid-growth sectors will show net upward shifts. At the same time, since regions compete for industries, some of them will be getting more or less of *any* given industry, whether it is growing nationally or not. This might be termed the *local-factor* effect. The regions that show net upward local-factor shifts will have gained because of their greater locational advantages for the operation of the given industries.

To measure these two effects, total employment for each state is broken down into its component industries for each of the Census 1-digit sectors listed in Table 9. The national growth rate for each industry within the state from the period 1939 to 1958 is applied to the state's 1939 employment data. The result represents the increase in employment which would come as the result of the "composition effect." This computed increase is then subtracted from the actual increase in that industry in the state between 1939 and 1958. The residual is the "local-factor effect." It represents the growth due to the fact that the industry in that state was growing more rapidly than—or (negatively) not as rapidly as—the national average for that industry. For example, take agricultural employment in California.

Nationally, agricultural employment declined 33.1 per cent between 1939 and 1958. After applying this reduction to 1939 agricultural employment in California, the result is compared with the actual change in agricultural employment in California between these two dates. The computed result was 141,951 jobs lower than the actual agricultural employment in California in 1958. Thus, California may be said to have had an increase in agricultural employment due to a local-factor effect equivalent to 141,951 jobs. Since California has more agricultural employment than the national average percentage change would provide for, other states necessarily would have absorbed a negative local-factor shift in agriculture to balance the California positive local-factor shift.

Total employment has been broken down into the ten component 1-digit employment categories in each of the 48 states and the local-factor net shifts and composition net shifts computed for each state between 1939 and 1958. The percentage distribution in local-factor net shifts in total employment appears in Figure 8. The percentage distribution of composition net shifts in total employment for the

Figure 8
Percentage Distribution of Local-Factor
Net Shifts in Total Employment, 1939-1958

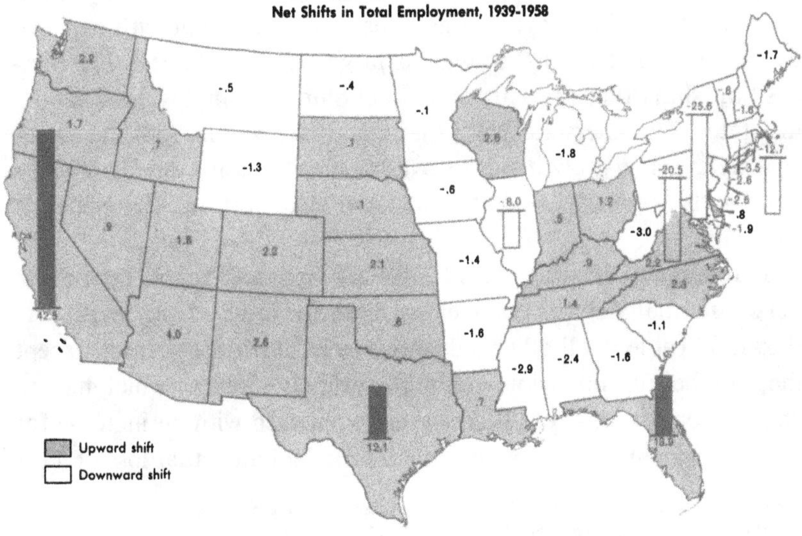

same period is presented in Figure 9.[2]

Figure 9
Percentage Distribution of Composition Net Shifts in Total Employment, 1939-1958

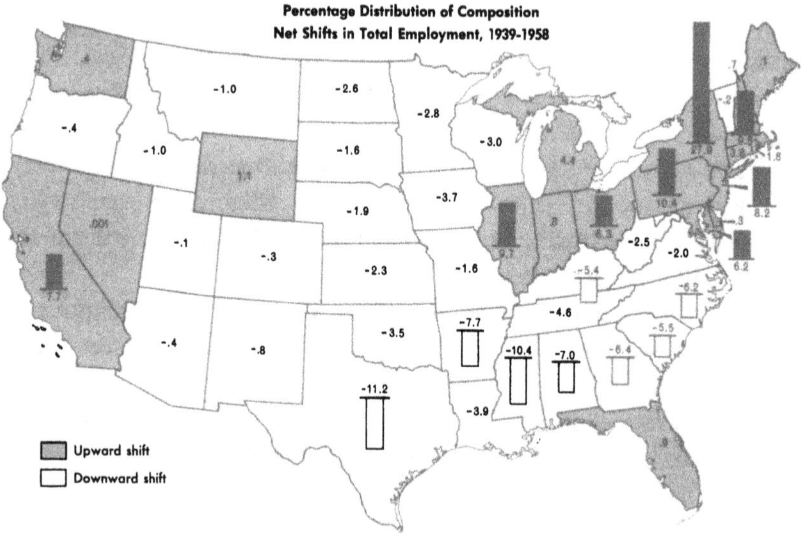

Those sectors in which employment changes greatly exceed, or fall short of, the national average are classified as rapid-growth or slow-growth industries; their behavior is largely responsible for the composition shifts that are part of the net shifts in employment among the states. The interstate shifts that take place within both the rapid-growth and slow-growth sectors over time account for the *local-factor* (or "within-industry") shifts that are also part of the net shift pattern.[3]

Throughout the entire period 1939-58, only mining and agriculture fell substantially below the average increase in all employment. (As shown in Table 9, all other industries were above the average except those in the transportation and public utilities category which had an employment increase of 37.2 per cent compared with an increase for all employment of 42.5 per cent.) Mining had an actual loss of 11.2

[2]The information in Figures 8 and 9 cannot be directly compared. It should be remembered that the figure shown for any one state is its percentage of the total upward shifts or the total downward shifts for the item being compared, whether the composition effect or the local-factor effect.

[3]A more detailed analysis of the composition and local-factor shifts is presented in the technical note at the end of this chapter.

per cent over the period and agriculture a loss of 33.1 per cent. It is not surprising, then, to find that the states that have a large proportion of their total employment in these two slow-growth sectors are those that are shown to have net downward composition shifts. Mississippi, which is one of these states, devoted nearly 75 per cent of its employment to agriculture and mining in 1939, as compared with 29 per cent for the nation as a whole. Similarly, in West Virginia almost 21 per cent of the total employment was in mining as compared with a national average of only 2 per cent. In contrast, New York, which shows a large net upward composition shift, devoted 93 per cent of its total employment in 1939 to rapid-growth sectors of employment, as compared with 70 per cent for the nation as a whole. Michigan, Massachusetts, New Jersey, and Connecticut derived most of their net upward composition shifts from a specialization in manufacturing, which accounted for 40 per cent or more of their employment, as compared with a national average of 23.5 per cent.

In order to arrive at more fundamental explanations of the differential growth patterns, a deeper look is needed at the factors relevant to both the composition and the local-factor effects. The composition effect raises this key question: *Why do some employment sectors of the national economy expand more than others?* The local-factor effect raises another key question: *Why does the same employment sector expand more rapidly in some regions than in others?*

An answer to these questions requires some knowledge of the reasons why one region may, for a particular activity, have access to inputs and markets superior to that of another region. It requires some knowledge of the significance of the spatial input-output relationships and of multiplier effects of the sort discussed in Chapter 2. As pointed out in that chapter, analysis of the composition effect can be accomplished through an investigation into national demand and supply factors and trends without consideration of the nature of regions other than to identify the locations of rapid-growth and slow-growth industries. However, little or no useful analysis of the local-factor effect is possible without taking into account modifications in regional input-output associations that represent changes in access for specific activities in specific regions.

Almost a third of the original study on which this book is based is devoted to the analysis of specific economic activities among regions for the period 1939-54. Even so, the coverage could by no means be complete. Here, in this condensed version, only a few of the case materials included in the parent study can be covered.

In Chapters 6, 7, and 8, three major sectors of the economy — mining, agriculture, and manufacturing — are examined for the broad changes they have shown over the period 1939-58, and in each case the contributions of the various industry components (the Census 2-digit employment categories) are considered. For a deeper look at these 2-digit industries (which entails an analysis of their 3-digit components), the following are selected for emphasis:

in mining — coal, because in analyzing the behavior of this industry many of the behavior patterns of its competitor, petroleum and natural gas, are highlighted;

in agriculture — livestock, because its behavior is linked with that of another large sector, feed grains;

in manufacturing — metal products and industrial organic chemicals, because analysis of these components sheds some light on the behavior of the primary metals, and the chemical products industry.

The fourth major sector of employment — service activities — is excluded from analysis here because little of the needed supplementary data are available for detailed analysis. The importance of this sector has been demonstrated by the growth and distribution figures for services employment shown in Tables 3 and 5. The service sector consists entirely of rapid-growth industries and thus contributes a tendency toward the net upward shift in employment for those regions that specialize in such activities (the Far West and Mountain states, Texas, Florida, and the states associated with the nodal centers of New York City, Boston, Baltimore-Washington, and Chicago).

By and large, it may be said that the changes in access that have brought about the shifts in service activities are essentially associated with regional changes in final demand. This is suggested by the extent to which employment in the major service industries is correlated with the number of persons within the states. The correlation between service employment and population is never perfect, even in retail trade. However, as shown in Table 10 (derived from the 1-digit components of total employment for each state in 1954), the correlation is extremely high for each of the service industries — even in the case of those like the finance, insurance, and real estate category and the transportation and public utility category which are to an important extent involved in serving business rather than the final consumer.

These service-population correlations contrast sharply with the situation in the case of mining and agriculture, where the resource tie is strong. The relatively high connection of manufacturing employment and population is one other indication of the relative importance of the market for most manufacturing activities.

Technical Note

An example of the way in which shift analysis is applied to one state's employment behavior may clarify the extensive use made of the technique in this analysis.

Between 1939 and 1958, California had an increase in total employment of 2,735,846 workers. If its employment had grown at the same percentage rate as for the country as a whole over these years, its increase would have been only some 894,064 workers. Thus, California can be said to have had a net upward shift in employment between 1939 and 1958 of 1,841,782 — the difference between the two figures. *This is the net employment shift.*

If the same technique is applied to each industry, instead of to only the total, the result is as shown for California in Table 11.

It can be seen from this table that every major industry in California experienced a greater increase in employment than it would have if each industry had grown at the national rate for that industry. The sum of these

Table 11. Illustration of the local-factor shift for selected states, 1939-58

Major industrial sectors	California	Texas	Pennsylvania	Georgia
Agriculture	+ 141,951	—164,189	+ 4,362	—143,959
Mining	— 255	+ 90,567	—110,501	+ 1,962
Construction	+ 96,462	— 4,250	— 19,949	— 10,509
Manufacturing	+ 610,407	+202,594	—281,905	+ 16,839
Transportation and public utilities	+ 99,997	+ 37,741	— 50,663	+ 7,416
Wholesale trade	+ 33,367	+ 34,314	— 5,769	+ 14,119
Retail trade	+ 155,781	+ 77,289	—100,033	+ 13,528
Finance, insurance and real estate	+ 48,352	+ 38,339	— 9,508	+ 13,673
Service and miscellaneous	+ 76,356	+ 21,324	— 35,194	— 13,949
Government	+ 303,603	+112,916	—147,101	+ 43,107
Total local-factor net shift in employment	+1,566,021	+446,645	—756,261	— 57,773

shifts gives the *total local-factor net shift* in employment for the state. But this total — 1,566,021 — is less than the total net shift in employment when calculated on the basis of the state's total expected rate of employment growth—the 1,841,782 wage jobs mentioned above. The difference—275,761 — is a result of the *composition effect* and it exists because not only did each industry in California grow more than the national average for the industry, but California's industry mix or composition was such that the number of workers employed in growth industries exceeded the national average. California, then, experienced an upward net shift in total employment because both the local-factor and composition effects in the major industries contributed to it.

Table 12. Illustration of total net employment shifts resulting from the local-factor effect and the composition effect for selected states, 1939-1958.

Total employment shift	California	Texas	Pennsylvania	Georgia
Net shift in total employment	+1,841,782	+ 45,513	—385,651	—287,224
Net local-factor (within industry) shift in total employment	+1,566,021	+446,645	—756,261	— 57,773
Net composition (industry growth) shift in total employment	+ 275,761	—401,132	+370,610	—229,451

Table 12 clarifies this result for California, and also shows what has happened to employment in three other states over the 1939-58 period. Texas experienced an upward net shift in total employment, but only because a very strong upward local-factor shift was sufficient to offset a significant downward composition shift — a reflection of this state's relative specialization in mining and agriculture. Pennsylvania reversed the experience of Texas. Its downward net employment shift took place because a strong downward local-factor shift was sufficient to offset a significant upward composition shift based upon relative specialization in manufacturing, trade, and services. In Georgia, the local-factor effect and the composition effect reinforced each other in generating a downward net shift in employment — a result largely due to a big downward shift in agriculture.

Looking again at Table 11, one can see how the employment situations for Texas, Pennsylvania, and Georgia were specified. The local-factor shifts shown for these states were derived in precisely the same way as were the shifts for California. First, the net upward or downward shift in each of the various employment sectors was computed. The net local-factor upward or downward shift in total employment for each of the states is the algebraic sum of these shifts in the component sectors.

Suppose that, by an extraordinary coincidence, none of the component sectors shown in Table 11 had any net upward or downward shift, it would follow that the local-factor net shift for each state would be zero. It would not follow, however, that there would be no net shift in total employment for these states because the composition effect remains as a source of shifting employment shares.

Table 13 presents the results of applying this type of analysis to each of the forty-eight states. It shows how the total employment shift for each state is divided between the composition and local-factor effect and how the local-factor effect in each is derived from the ten broad industry components[4]. Thus, it can be seen how Florida, the Far Western states, the southern Mountain states (Colorado and Utah), Arizona and Delaware, had net upward shifts in employment almost entirely because their important industry sectors were growing at a greater rate than the national average for these sectors; and how Maine and New Hampshire experienced the reverse situation. In contrast, Maryland's total net upward shift is largely accounted for by the state's specialization in industry sectors that were growing at a faster rate than the average for all industries. And specialization in industry sectors that had been declining nationally, or growing at a below-average rate for the nation as a whole, is the major factor in the total net downward shifts shown by Minnesota, Iowa, North and South Dakota, and Nebraska in the Plains region, and by all the Southeastern states except Florida, Virginia, and West Virginia.

In other states the net employment shift reflects both the composition and local-factor effects, the one tending either to offset or support the other.

[4]This table was prepared by one of the authors of the parent study, Edgar S. Dunn, Jr., as part of the working materials for a further study he is making of regional economic growth.

Table 13. State total, composition, and local-factor net shifts in employment and the industry components of the local-factor shifts, 1939-1958

(absolute and per cent)*

State	Total employment net shift	Composition net shift	Local-factor net shift	1-Digit components of local-factor shift in employment								
				Agriculture	Mining	Construction	Manufacturing	Transportation and public utilities	Wholesale trade	Retail trade	Finance, insurance and real estate	Service and miscellaneous	Government
New England													
Maine	— 58,624	+ 4,855	— 63,479	+ 14,416	— 88	— 2,584	— 41,775	— 4,037	— 44	— 6,958	— 559	— 7,454	— 14,396
		7.10	92.89	15.62	0.09	2.80	45.25	4.37	0.05	7.54	0.61	8.07	15.59
New Hampshire	— 32,906	+ 24,442	— 57,348	— 2,047	— 58	— 5,780	— 22,842	— 1,910	+ 1,665	— 3,496	+ 1,154	— 6,006	— 18,028
		29.88	70.11	3.25	0.09	9.18	36.27	3.03	2.64	5.55	1.83	9.53	28.62
Vermont	— 31,532	— 8,359	— 23,173	+ 582	— 752	— 2,346	— 9,957	— 2,178	— 366	— 3,948	+ 538	— 483	— 4,263
		26.51	73.49	2.29	2.96	9.23	39.18	8.57	1.44	15.53	2.12	1.90	16.77
Massachusetts	— 129,204	+339,201	— 468,405	— 10,512	— 439	— 6,512	—242,108	— 22,867	— 15,822	— 78,501	— 4,703	— 4,415	— 82,526
		42.00	58.00	2.24	0.09	1.39	51.69	4.88	3.38	16.76	1.00	0.94	17.62
Rhode Island	— 63,764	+ 64,885	— 128,649	— 912	— 86	— 8,207	— 88,778	— 1,938	— 276	— 14,038	— 773	— 4,656	— 8,985
		33.53	66.47	0.71	0.07	6.38	69.01	1.51	0.21	10.91	0.60	3.62	6.98
Connecticut	+ 38,883	+135,234	— 96,351	— 4,854	+ 197	— 4,513	— 75,775	+ 2,607	+ 8,257	— 4,455	+ 1,341	— 5,160	— 13,996
		58.39	41.61	4.01	0.16	3.72	62.54	2.15	6.81	3.68	1.11	4.26	11.55
Middle Atlantic													
New York	+ 50,772	+996,614	— 945,842	— 26,820	+ 1,995	— 89,658	—105,449	— 95,045	—101,895	—126,860	—199,309	— 89,005	—113,769
		51.31	48.69	2.82	0.21	9.44	11.10	10.01	10.73	13.36	20.98	9.37	11.98
New Jersey	+ 196,059	+291,400	— 95,341	+ 3,560	— 48	— 8,888	— 92,085	— 879	+ 25,537	+ 4,256	— 12,687	+ 2,930	— 17,037
		75.35	24.65	2.12	0.03	5.29	54.84	0.52	15.21	2.53	7.55	1.75	10.15
Pennsylvania	— 385,651	+370,610	— 756,261	+ 4,362	—110,501	— 19,949	—281,905	— 50,663	— 5,769	—100,033	— 9,508	— 35,194	—147,101
		32.89	67.11	0.57	14.44	2.61	36.85	6.62	0.75	13.08	1.24	4.60	19.23
Delaware	+ 41,766	+ 11,574	+ 30,192	+ 2,742	+ 11	— 1,169	+ 18,168	+ 1,608	+ 2,410	+ 3,140	— 21	+ 1,790	+ 1,513
		27.71	72.29	8.42	0.03	3.59	55.78	4.94	7.40	9.64	0.06	5.49	4.65
Maryland and D.C.	+ 150,494	+220,449	— 69,955	+ 5,789	— 1,042	— 20,772	— 22,524	— 7,523	— 6,420	— 4,371	+ 3,412	— 8,635	— 7,869
		75.91	24.09	6.55	1.18	23.51	25.49	8.51	7.27	4.95	3.86	9.77	8.91
Great Lakes													
Ohio	+ 269,219	+225,190	+ 44,029	+ 27,936	— 4,389	+ 23,287	— 33,485	— 4,128	+ 10,145	— 13,872	+ 5,107	+ 50,912	— 17,484
		83.65	16.35	14.65	2.30	12.21	17.55	2.16	5.32	7.27	2.68	26.69	9.17
Indiana	+ 45,488	+ 27,187	+ 18,301	+ 56,886	— 2,504	+ 2,761	— 15,627	— 7,812	+ 7,751	— 3,814	+ 2,315	— 12,812	— 8,843
		59.77	40.23	46.96	2.07	2.28	12.90	6.45	6.40	3.15	1.91	10.58	7.30
Illinois	+ 52,596	+347,849	— 295,253	+ 42,831	— 12,505	+ 17,968	— 77,978	— 25,580	— 18,788	— 58,977	— 65,728	— 67,520	— 28,976
		54.09	45.91	10.27	3.00	4.31	18.71	6.14	4.51	14.15	15.77	16.20	6.95
Michigan	+ 92,091	+156,693	— 64,602	+ 29,343	— 175	— 11,203	—153,211	+ 18,839	+ 10,262	— 4,333	+ 4,658	+ 9,156	+ 32,062
		70.81	29.19	10.74	0.06	4.10	56.07	6.89	3.75	1.59	1.70	3.35	11.73
Wisconsin	— 12,482	—108,883	+ 96,401	+ 74,448	+ 1,545	— 7,355	+ 14,536	— 48	+ 5,844	+ 333	+ 1,498	+ 4,335	+ 1,265
		53.04	46.96	66.95	1.39	6.61	13.07	0.04	5.25	0.30	1.35	3.90	1.14
Southeast													
Virginia	+ 10,033	— 70,360	+ 80,393	+ 18,273	+ 368	— 1,524	+ 3,904	+ 3,781	— 14,082	+ 30,558	+ 14,376	+ 1,127	+ 23,612
		46.67	53.33	16.37	0.33	1.37	3.50	3.39	12.62	27.38	12.88	1.01	21.16
West Virginia	— 197,744	— 88,637	— 109,107	— 19,831	— 26,793	— 7,114	— 28,818	— 2,041	— 1,993	— 6,729	+ 554	— 575	— 15,767
		44.82	55.17	17.99	24.31	6.45	26.15	1.85	1.81	6.11	0.50	0.52	14.31
North Carolina	— 135,638	—221,901	+ 86,263	+ 68,032	+ 1,889	— 990	— 27,109	+ 17,649	— 21,660	+ 18,353	+ 9,403	+ 3,658	+ 17,038
		72.01	27.99	36.62	1.02	0.53	14.59	9.50	11.66	9.88	5.06	1.97	9.17
South Carolina	— 236,277	—195,345	— 40,932	— 52,668	+ 266	— 1,206	— 3,078	+ 1,468	+ 4,657	+ 1,928	+ 10,127	— 10,596	+ 8,170
		82.68	17.32	55.93	0.28	1.28	3.27	1.56	4.95	2.05	10.75	11.25	8.68
Georgia	— 287,224	—229,451	— 57,773	—143,959	+ 1,962	— 10,509	+ 16,839	+ 7,416	+ 14,119	+ 13,528	+ 13,673	— 13,949	+ 43,107
		79.89	20.11	51.59	0.70	3.77	6.03	2.66	5.06	4.85	4.90	5.00	15.45
Florida	+ 544,352	+ 32,465	+ 511,887	+ 24,353	+ 3,565	+ 61,926	+ 65,890	+ 27,015	+ 15,277	+110,203	+ 40,052	+ 83,617	+ 79,989
		5.96	94.04	4.76	0.70	12.10	12.87	5.28	2.98	21.53	7.82	16.33	15.63
Kentucky	— 158,168	—192,142	+ 33,974	+ 10,945	— 11,811	— 10,340	+ 35,536	— 4,319	+ 866	+ 4,260	+ 4,409	+ 16,114	— 11,686
		84.97	15.03	[illegible]	10.71	9.37	32.22	3.92	0.79	3.86	4.00	14.61	10.60

Tennessee	− 112,722	−162,815	+ 50,093	− 10,191	− 2,225	+ 783	+ 24,914	+ 2,259	+ 8,213	+ 7,603	+ 12,019	− 4,388	+ 11,104
		76.47	23.53	12.18	2.66	0.93	29.77	2.70	9.81	9.08	14.36	5.24	13.27
Alabama	− 340,092	−250,580	− 89,512	−153,101	− 11,978	− 60	+ 12,393	− 1,276	+ 9,110	+ 11,991	+ 11,287	+ 3,594	+ 28,528
		73.68	26.32	62.92	4.92	0.02	5.09	0.52	3.74	4.93	4.64	1.48	11.72
Mississippi	− 476,742	−370,390	− 106,352	−116,425	+ 4,607	− 9,710	+ 21,669	− 1,179	+ 3,591	+ 2,521	+ 5,830	− 1,428	− 15,828
		77.69	22.31	63.69	2.52	5.31	11.85	0.65	1.96	1.38	3.19	0.78	8.66
Arkansas	− 333,996	−276,800	− 57,196	− 65,475	− 487	− 3,918	+ 18,466	− 3,392	+ 1,079	+ 439	+ 4,449	+ 2,688	− 11,044
		82.87	17.12	58.75	0.44	3.51	16.57	3.04	0.97	0.39	3.99	2.41	9.91
Louisiana	− 112,752	−138,995	+ 26,243	− 65,023	+ 35,679	+ 18,217	− 10,828	+ 14,180	+ 4,439	+ 10,017	+ 11,806	+ 1,753	+ 6,003
		84.12	15.88	36.54	20.05	10.24	6.09	7.97	2.49	5.63	6.63	0.99	3.37
Plains													
Minnesota	− 105,020	−101,167	− 3,853	+ 41,862	+ 9,890	− 7,693	+ 44,998	+ 225	− 8,100	− 20,323	− 1,199	− 6,360	− 57,153
		96.33	3.67	21.16	5.00	3.89	22.75	0.11	4.09	10.27	0.61	3.22	28.89
Iowa	− 157,015	−133,469	− 23,546	+ 62,463	− 2,660	− 16,744	+ 18,381	− 8,647	− 2,428	− 26,668	+ 417	− 13,354	− 34,306
		85.00	15.00	33.57	1.43	9.00	9.88	4.65	1.30	14.33	0.22	7.18	18.44
Missouri	− 108,595	− 57,449	− 51,146	+ 36,118	− 1,407	− 3,055	+ 8,101	+ 3,564	− 24,770	− 15,843	− 7,047	− 24,634	− 22,173
		52.92	47.10	24.62	0.96	2.08	5.52	2.43	16.88	10.80	4.80	16.79	15.11
North Dakota	− 109,184	− 94,071	− 15,113	− 5,257	+ 993	+ 3,731	− 346	− 59	− 1,819	+ 86	+ 1,011	− 3,429	− 10,024
		86.16	13.84	19.65	3.71	13.95	1.29	0.22	6.80	0.32	3.78	12.82	37.47
South Dakota	− 56,201	− 58,234	+ 2,033	+ 20,534	− 28	− 584	+ 609	− 1,350	+ 157	− 1,327	+ 984	− 628	− 16,334
		96.63	3.37	48.27	0.07	1.37	1.43	3.17	0.37	3.12	2.31	1.48	38.40
Nebraska	− 62,331	− 66,853	+ 4,522	+ 32,719	+ 1,653	− 3,191	+ 14,064	− 926	− 4,044	− 9,911	+ 3,611	− 5,926	− 23,527
		93.66	6.34	32.86	1.66	3.20	14.12	0.93	4.06	9.95	3.63	5.95	23.63
Kansas	− 5,136	− 80,919	+ 75,783	+ 27,694	+ 3,937	+ 9,155	+ 46,527	− 938	− 100	− 1,905	+ 3,133	+ 455	− 12,175
		51.64	48.36	26.12	3.71	8.63	43.89	0.88	0.09	1.80	2.95	0.43	11.48
Southwest													
Oklahoma	− 102,480	−126,497	+ 24,017	− 1,532	+ 12,849	+ 1,671	+ 29,187	+ 5,195	+ 2,049	− 8,458	+ 4,279	− 22,775	+ 1,552
		84.04	15.96	1.71	14.35	1.87	32.59	5.80	2.29	9.45	4.78	25.43	1.73
Texas	+ 45,513	−401,132	+ 446,645	−164,189	+ 90,567	− 4,250	+202,594	+ 37,741	+ 34,314	+ 77,289	+ 38,339	+ 21,324	+112,916
		48.48	52.68	20.95	11.56	0.54	25.86	4.82	4.38	9.86	4.89	2.72	14.41
New Mexico	+ 68,984	− 28,766	+ 97,750	+ 8,869	+ 10,230	+ 10,612	+ 13,363	+ 6,555	+ 4,253	+ 13,538	+ 5,968	+ 5,395	+ 18,967
		22.74	77.26	9.07	10.47	10.86	13.67	6.71	4.35	13.85	6.11	5.52	19.40
Arizona	+ 132,235	− 14,487	+ 146,722	+ 16,141	+ 5,982	+ 16,043	+ 26,990	+ 6,685	+ 9,598	+ 24,392	+ 9,114	+ 9,423	+ 22,354
		8.99	91.01	11.00	4.08	10.93	18.39	4.56	6.54	16.62	6.21	6.42	15.23
Mountain													
Montana	− 54,174	− 34,481	− 19,693	− 573	− 2,251	− 2,472	− 650	− 3,337	+ 889	− 1,849	+ 2,387	+ 1,228	− 13,065
		63.65	36.35	2.00	7.84	8.61	2.26	11.63	3.10	6.44	8.32	4.28	45.52
Idaho	− 12,129	− 37,368	+ 25,239	+ 14,968	− 490	+ 2,789	+ 6,029	+ 2,292	+ 383	+ 1,283	+ 2,465	− 27	− 4,453
		59.69	40.31	42.55	1.39	7.93	17.14	6.51	1.09	3.65	7.01	0.08	12.66
Wyoming	− 9,795	+ 39,750	− 49,545	+ 560	+ 3,186	− 915	− 1,160	− 3,340	+ 555	+ 596	+ 1,170	− 49,642	− 555
		44.51	55.48	0.91	5.17	1.48	1.88	5.41	0.90	0.97	1.90	80.48	0.90
Colorado	+ 69,781	− 10,670	+ 80,451	+ 4,349	+ 1,204	+ 3,267	+ 23,644	+ 4,748	+ 4,881	+ 5,138	+ 5,763	+ 8,704	+ 18,753
		11.71	88.29	5.41	1.50	4.06	29.39	5.90	6.06	6.39	7.16	10.82	23.31
Utah	+ 63,052	− 3,921	+ 66,973	+ 11,796	+ 4,275	+ 4,577	+ 11,097	+ 486	+ 1,987	+ 4,893	+ 4,303	+ 5,683	+ 17,876
		5.53	94.47	17.61	6.38	6.83	16.57	0.73	2.97	7.31	6.42	8.49	26.69
Far West													
Washington	+ 93,347	+ 12,354	+ 80,993	+ 19,272	− 1,815	− 6,675	+ 34,531	− 11,350	− 1,592	+ 5,900	+ 5,665	+ 13,816	+ 23,241
		13.23	86.77	15.56	1.47	5.39	27.88	9.16	1.29	4.76	4.57	11.15	18.76
Oregon	+ 48,957	− 12,584	+ 61,541	+ 19,219	− 123	+ 5,366	+ 10,279	+ 1,298	+ 2,995	+ 4,639	+ 4,671	+ 7,037	+ 6,160
		16.98	83.02	31.11	0.20	8.68	16.64	2.10	4.85	7.51	7.56	11.39	9.97
California	+1,841,782	+275,761	+1,566,021	+141,951	− 255	+ 96,462	+610,407	+ 99,997	+ 33,367	+155,781	+ 48,352	+ 76,356	+303,603
		14.97	85.03	9.06	0.02	6.16	38.97	6.38	2.13	9.94	3.09	4.87	19.38
Nevada	+ 32,478	+ 489	+ 31,989	+ 355	− 1,935	+ 1,273	+ 2,381	+ 1,154	+ 1,321	+ 4,006	+ 1,897	+ 17,050	+ 4,487
		1.51	98.49	0.99	5.40	3.55	6.64	3.22	3.68	11.17	5.29	47.55	12.51

*First line for each state is absolute shift, second line per cent shift. Percentages are based upon sum without regard to sign, in order to avoid the extreme distortions of the algebraic sum.

6. Changes in Mining Employment

A region's access to important inputs and markets and its adaptability to changing technology, organization, and demand are the variables that play a dominant role in governing the direction and location of industrial activities over time and, in particular, are responsible for the highly fluid characteristic of regional economic growth in the United States. There is no absolute scale for measuring a region's "access" characteristics or its exhibited development. These take on meaning only as the performance of specific activities in one region are compared with those of other regions and of the nation as a whole.

The mining, agricultural, and manufacturing activities examined in this and the next two chapters are selected not necessarily for the size of their contribution to the total national economy, but because they highlight varying effects upon regional structures. Limitations of space impose restrictions on the number of industry components that can be included here. Enough are examined, however, to provide a general idea of the changes in regional economic activity that have occurred over the last two decades, and some understanding of the forces that have brought them into being.

In this chapter, the mining sector's influence upon the shifts in regional employment over the period 1939-58 is highlighted. The shifts in employment within one of mining's subcategories are then looked at and factors that have contributed to these shifts are discussed. Thus, the analysis narrows from the broadest category, total employment, to the 1-digit category, mining, to a 2-digit component of mining, coal mining.

Mining Employment

Mining is the smallest of the main employment sectors, accounting for only 1.3 per cent of total national employment. It does, however, provide industry with much of its basic material inputs, and it is highly localized. Therefore, whether considered as a whole or for each of its component sectors (coal, crude petroleum and natural gas, metals, and nonmetallic minerals), mining can be quite important in explaining the economic behavior of regions and localities that are dependent on it for employment.

Table 14. Mining employment as percentage of total employment, 1939 and 1958, for states where mining employment exceeded the national average in 1939

State	1939 Per cent	1958 Per cent	State	1939 Per cent	1958 Per cent
United States average	2.0	1.3			
West Virginia	20.9	12.8	Oklahoma	5.3	5.5
Nevada	13.7	3.4	Colorado	4.6	2.7
Wyoming	7.8	8.3	Alabama	3.2	1.4
Kentucky	7.5	4.2	Idaho	3.0	1.8
Arizona	7.4	4.6	Kansas	2.7	2.2
Utah	7.2	5.0	Texas	2.6	4.8
Pennsylvania	7.0	1.9	Virginia	2.5	1.6
Montana	6.2	3.8	Louisiana[a]	1.6	5.1
New Mexico	5.7	6.4			

[a] Louisiana is included although its employment was below average in 1939. During the subsequent 19 years its concentration on oil produced the high figure indicated in 1958.

Mining employment in 1958 amounted to 734,994 persons as compared with 827,410 in 1939 – a decline of 11 per cent. Some idea of the effects of this on the states where mining is, in varying degrees, an important part of the economy is shown in Table 14. Since 1939, only five of the seventeen states listed have increased the ratio of mining employment to total employment. The growth of petroleum and natural gas accounts for the expansion in Texas, Louisiana, and Oklahoma; increases in metal mining have boosted somewhat mining employment in New Mexico and Wyoming.

The declining share of mining employment, and the accompanying decline in mining's share of the gross national product, basically are results of the increasing importance of other primary and intermediate inputs in the sequences of industrial production. Mineral-saving developments in technology since World War I have led to increasing use of scrap metals and minerals substitutes. The decline is intensified by greater mechanization and other technical and managerial improvements leading to larger productive capacity of the labor force. Another contributing factor is the separation from mining of many of its former functions. The trend in recent years, for example, is for mining engineers and financial services to be covered under "business services." Similarly, some beneficiation processes have been so segmented that they are now classified as "manufacturing processes."

The over-all picture of mining employment – summed up in the net shifts in Figure 10 – shows distinct changes in the relative positions of the states over the 1939-58 period. The net employment shifts among the states, in fact, amounted to ±196,847 workers. This is 24 per cent of the 1939 mining employment figure and a

Figure 10
Percentage Distribution of Net Shifts in Mining Employment, 1939-1958

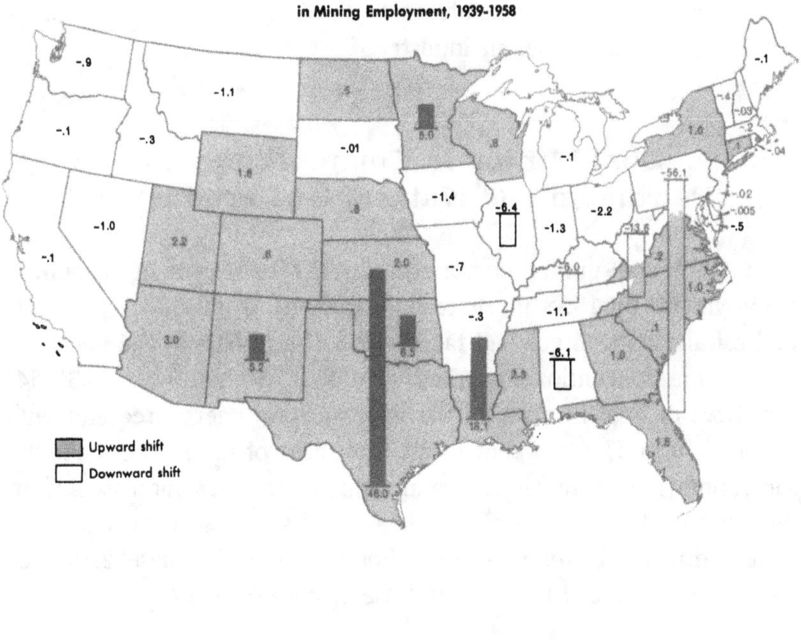

larger proportion of the absolute changes than in any other of the major employment sectors.

Perhaps the most striking feature of the picture is the way in which it explains the behavior of two areas – one of major growth in total employment, the other of major relative decline. The Southwest, particularly Texas, and Louisiana clearly have owed a great deal of their growth to minerals production, chiefly of oil and gas and their geological associates, sulfur and salt. Declines in coal mining have brought about the marked downward shifts in mining employment in Pennsylvania, West Virginia, and Kentucky, which together produce 72 per cent of the nation's coal output.

The wide disparities in rates of growth in mining employment among the states are seen most clearly when the major segments of mining are looked at separately. Table 15 gives a rough idea of the size of the shifts and how each of the mining subsectors has departed from the changes for the sector as a whole. Net shifts among the states in metal mining employment, for example, were nearly eight times as large between 1939 and 1958 as the absolute change of metal mining employment in the nation as a whole (compare Column 7 with Column 5). But, while coal mining for the nation declined by 29 per cent, net state shifts amounted to only 14 per cent of the absolute change. In terms of the numbers of workers involved (Column 7 as per cent of Column 1) the largest net shift, of 52 per cent, was in the petroleum industry.

Coal Mining in Competition with Petroleum and Natural Gas Production

In 1939, coal mining comprised almost 60 per cent of all mining employment; by 1958 its share had dropped to only 28.6 per cent, and oil and natural gas had taken over a large part of the newer as well as the conventional markets of coal. Over the years 1939-54, the share of coal in meeting the nation's total energy requirements dropped from 51.4 per cent to 29.3 per cent of total BTU's. At the same time the share of petroleum and natural gas increased from 44.9 per cent to 66.8 per cent. In many uses these energy sources were a direct substitute for coal. For example, the dieselization of locomotives reduced the railways' use of coal from 120 million tons

Table 15. Relative importance of net employment shifts in mining, 1939-1958

2-Digit mining categories	Employment				Absolute change 1939-58	Percentage increase (Col. 5 as per cent of Col. 1)	Total net shift 1939-58	Net shift as per cent of:	
	1939	Per cent	1958	Per cent				Absolute change	1939 employment
	(1)	(2)	(3)	(4)	(5)	(6)	(7)	(8)	(9)
All mining employment	827,410	100.0	734,994	100.0	— 92,416	— 11.2	± 196,847	± 213.0	± 23.8
Crude petroleum and natural gas	151,939	18.4	317,115	43.1	165,176	108.7	± 78,826	± 47.7	± 51.9
Nonmetallic minerals	(95,184)	11.5	115,096	15.7	19,912	20.9	± 20,393	± 102.4	± 21.4
Metal mining	(95,767)	11.6	92,441	12.6	— 3,326	— 3.5	± 25,950	± 780.2	± 27.1
Coal mining	483,567	58.5	210,342	28.6	—273,225	— 56.5	± 37,340	± 13.7	± 7.7

Note: Parentheses indicate estimates.

to 17 million tons between 1945 and 1955. Oil and natural gas have also claimed a large share of the heating market and the electric utility market. While the absolute amount of coal used in generating electric power increased substantially during the period, the share of coal in this important market dropped from 81.7 per cent in 1945 to 65.6 per cent in 1955, and to 55 per cent in 1957.

Another reason for the relative decline of coal in the energy market is that oil (and the new oil technology) generated new energy sources and energy markets, notably the internal combustion engine, in which coal was not a reasonable technological substitute. Developments in coal technology have also contributed to the decline. The average amount of coal burned to produce one kilowatt-hour of electrical energy in the United States was 6.4 pounds in 1902, 3.0 pounds in 1920, and 1.2 pounds in 1950.

Interstate Shifts in Coal Mining

While employment in coal mining declined generally, the impact was far from uniform among the states. There were significant interstate shifts in shares of coal mining employment, with West Virginia, Virginia, and Kentucky maintaining their employment rates far above the national average and with Pennsylvania and Illinois experiencing declines far beyond the "expected" level. Here we have an industry in which immobile resource inputs make resource "access" a major factor in the regional distribution of activity. On the other hand, there are sufficient alternative sources of the same input to make market access an important consideration in the distribution of the industry. Further, the existence of a major substitute product can modify the dimensions of market access considerably.

Interregional shifts in coal mining are directly tied to changes in these factors. On the input side, resource depletion has undoubtedly exerted some influence. The shift out of Pennsylvania into the mid-Appalachian fields has arisen in part from the fact that many of the most productive seams have been exploited to the point where mid-Appalachian seams formerly of lower quality have become competitive. The wholesale change in fuels for home heating, from anthracite to oil, gas, and powdered coal, is a large factor here, in view of the fact that Pennsylvania was the chief producer of anthracite. Mechanization has had an important influence on anthracite and other coal mining. It has so altered the comparative advantage of deposits that many, given present demand and technology, have been redefined out of existence as an economic resource, and for others, profitable levels of exploitation have been sharply modified.

Labor costs may be yet another factor. Since labor represents 76 per cent of the purchased inputs for the coal industry, its rising costs may, in some fields, have submerged production below the margin of economic exploitation. This could be a contributing factor leading to a maximizing of production in those fields where output per man-hour tends to be the greatest.

The combined influence of these factors affecting resource access seems to have increased the importance of the mid-Appalachian states relative to other coal-producing regions.

In a similar way, interregional changes in relative access to markets have influenced the shifts. The substitution of oil for coal in the power market has been regionally concentrated, as is shown in Figure 11. In general, oil dominates the power market west of the Mississippi, and coal that east of the Mississippi. Thus coal has succeeded in holding this market in the areas with greatest access to prime coal sources and has lost out in the areas with greatest access to oil. The fact that the substitution of oil for coal is not equally feasible in every region is an element working in favor of coal production in the mid-Appalachian area. And there is another reason why the eastern coal areas have been less vulnerable to market loss through substitution. This is the area where the nation's manufacturing is concentrated, and it is in the manufacturing sectors that coal has had the greatest success in retaining its market. The portion of total output that goes to manufacturing is about three times greater for coal than for oil and gas.

Table 16, which gives data for 1947, indicates the considerable degree to which coal is successful in retaining its markets in manufacturing even in areas where its competitive position is weakest. In Texas, twelve of the twenty 2-digit manufacturing groups used coal and coke for 20 per cent or more of their energy requirements (and seven for more than 50 per cent). In contrast, oil failed to penetrate the manufacturing markets in West Virginia and showed only moderate penetration in Pennsylvania despite the fact that pipelines and

Figure 11
Relative Use of Coal and of Oil
or Natural Gas by Steam Electric Plants,
1960, by State

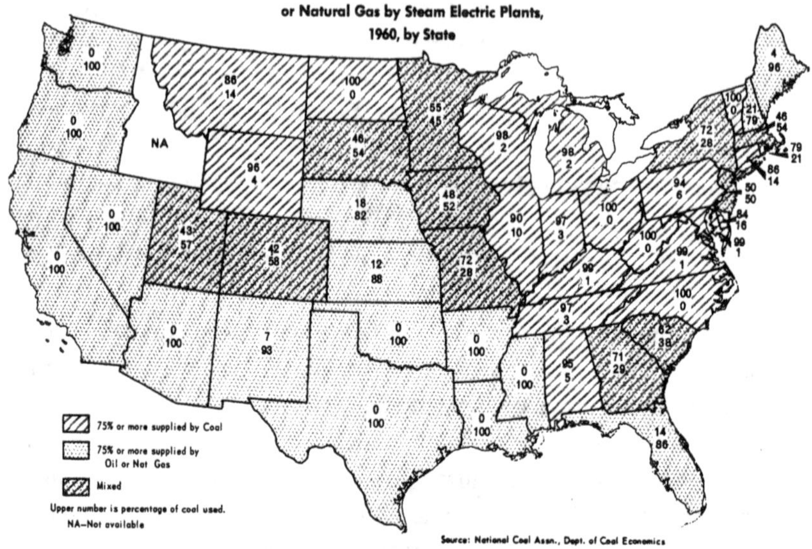

ocean transport give Pennsylvania favorable access to oil and gas fuels. Primary metals and machinery rely almost entirely on coal even in the heart of oil's competitive stronghold. Miscellaneous manufacturing and food products also continue to be strong coal users.

One further change in the market had an important effect on the regional changes in coal production and employment during the 1939-54 period. A sizable part of the output of the coal industry went to export. Between 1939 and 1954 these exports tripled, though they have since declined with the expanded output of European coal fields. The coal fields with most favorable access to ocean shipping are located in West Virginia and Virginia; this helps to explain the strong relative showing in these states.

Despite the serious loss of markets suffered by the coal mining industry, it should not be assumed that the resultant regional and national trends exhibited will necessarily continue. Energy is one of the fastest growing segments of the economy and the price trends of gas and oil are now starting to favor coal after working against it for more than thirty years. In addition, new technology is making coal burning more efficient. Public utility markets in New England, the Southeast, and the big metropolitan markets of New York City and Philadelphia have, in fact, already started to return to coal. Add to this trend the prospects that may develop out of carbonization and gas synthesis, coal pipelines, etc., the prospects for coal may very well improve.

Table 16. Relative use of coal and coke and of oil and natural gas in manufacturing in Pennsylvania, West Virginia, and Texas, by industry, 1947

2-Digit manufacturing categories	Coal and coke			Oil and natural gas		
	W. Va.	Penna.	Texas	W. Va.	Penna.	Texas
			(per cent)			
Food and kindred products	99.2	83.5	59.8	.8	16.5	39.4
Tobacco manufacturing	—	69.8	—	—	30.2	—
Textile mill products	99.7	77.2	29.3	.3	22.8	70.6
Apparel and related	99.8	79.3	—	.1	20.7	99.6
Lumber and products	82.7	74.7	28.2	17.3	25.1	70.9
Furniture and fixtures	100.0	89.8	68.9	—	10.5	31.4
Paper and allied products	100.0	90.6	—	—	9.4	99.3
Printing and publishing	87.3	82.2	55.5	12.6	18.2	43.4
Chemical and allied products	99.8	82.7	19.6	.2	17.3	79.9
Petroleum and coal products	95.9	86.8	—	3.2	11.7	99.7
Rubber plants	—	13.4	—	—	17.3	—
Leather and leather products	100.0	95.5	—	—	4.5	99.7
Stone, clay and glass	96.9	91.0	31.5	3.1	4.7	68.3
Primary metals products	91.7	89.6	82.2	8.1	10.3	17.8
Fabricated metals products	99.3	75.9	44.5	.7	24.0	55.1
Machinery (exc. electrical)	93.7	82.2	98.0	6.3	23.8	1.9
Electrical machinery	99.9	93.0	97.4	—	7.0	2.2
Transportation equipment	—	51.4	2.1	—	12.4	97.7
Instruments and related	—	74.2	—	—	23.4	99.1
Miscellaneous manufacturing	97.8	79.6	67.5	2.2	19.1	32.4

7. Changes in Agriculture

The dramatic decline in farm employment is a testimony to the sweeping changes that have industrialized the American economy since the turn of the century. Farms have become larger, fewer, and more mechanized; and the trend is continuing. For example, during the 1954-59 period covered by the 1959 farm census, the number of farms declined by 18 per cent, while the total amount of land used for farming decreased by only 3 per cent. At the same time, farm population as a whole has decreased. In fact, today it numbers only slightly more than it did during the Civil War, while farm output increased by about three and a half times between 1870 and 1957.

The Influence of Farm Employment upon Total Employment

Some of the regional effects of developments within agriculture, a major "slow-growth" sector of the economy, are seen in Table 17, which lists the twenty-nine states where the share of agricultural employment in 1939 was above the average for the nation. The declines shown between that year and 1958 have been largely responsible for the net composition effects in total employment that were shown by many of these states in Figure 9. Agriculture's share of the labor force of the nation declined by 53.1 per cent over these years.

Several long-term trends in supply and demand have contributed to these developments. First, on the supply side, there has been a pronounced trend for agriculture to cover fewer economic activities than formerly. Technological advances and increased specialization have led to many agricultural activities being taken over by manufacturing and the service sectors.

Table 17. Agricultural employment as percentage of total employment, 1939 and 1958, for states where agricultural employment exceeded the national average in 1939

State	1939	1958	State	1939	1958
United States average	27.5	12.9			
Mississippi	74.3	42.7	New Mexico	46.0	19.4
Arkansas	70.1	40.8	Iowa	45.6	31.6
North Dakota	68.3	45.6	Kansas	42.8	24.1
South Dakota	57.6	42.6	Montana	42.4	24.7
South Carolina	56.3	27.8	Minnesota	40.0	24.0
Alabama	54.6	18.1	Wyoming	36.0	19.0
Georgia	50.4	17.1	Virginia	35.9	18.3
Idaho	49.1	31.0	Vermont	35.1	21.0
Kentucky	48.8	28.3	Arizona	34.8	14.7
North Carolina	46.9	28.4	Wisconsin	34.5	21.5
Texas	46.9	15.9	Missouri	32.7	18.7
Oklahoma	46.8	24.8	Oregon	31.4	16.9
Louisiana	46.5	17.4	Colorado	30.0	13.1
Tennessee	46.2	23.0	West Virginia	28.1	14.4
Nebraska	46.1	30.7			

Second, the value-added factor helps to explain the relative decline of agriculture. The more extended fabrication that agricultural products undergo before reaching the final consumer generally adds to aggregate output without a commensurate increase in agricultural output.

Third, as with manufacturing and, to a lesser degree, mining, great increases in worker productivity, caused by improved technology, have helped bring about a relative decline in the importance of agricultural employment.

Fourth, on the demand side, consumption of farm products as a whole, and especially of food products, does not increase markedly as income rises. Expenditures for food at retail stores and restaurants have been increasing at a rate more or less proportionate to increases in income, but these expenditures cover services of processing and distribution as well as food. It is these services that have been increasing with rising per capita income, rather than consumption of farm products. Agriculture's share of total demand declines progressively as incomes and total demand rise.

Fifth, there has been a long-run decline in agriculture's share of American exports. Abnormal war demands have only briefly interrupted this consistent trend over several decades.

Sixth, for a number of agricultural products there has been sharp competition from synthetic and natural substitutes of nonagricultural origin. The case of synthetic fibers is illustrative.

As a consequence of these long-term trends, the regions that have depended largely on agriculture – the Southeast, Plains, and northern Mountain regions – have tended to lose out relative to regions with better access to manufacturing markets and basic intermediate inputs. Nevertheless, Figure 12 shows that in spite of the generally depressing effect of agricultural specialization, some regions – the Far West and Southern Mountain states and Indiana, for example – did increase their share of the nation's declining agricultural employment. On the other hand, conspicuous downward shifts in agricultural employment took place in the states of the Deep South and in Montana.

Measuring the Change in Value of Agricultural Products Sold

To look at the component segments of agriculture which together account for the interregional shifts that have taken place, it is necessary to depart from the use of employment as the basic measure of economic change. This is because statistics on farm employment are complicated by variations in reporting the employed time of workers. In its place, "value of agricultural products sold" is taken as the measure for agricultural change and the period examined is 1940-54.

The westward movement of agriculture is shown more clearly by the state-by-state shifts in shares of the value of all farm products sold (Figure 13) than by the data for agricultural employment (Figure 12), but, in general, the two measures tell a similar story.[1] Some 88

[1]The marked discrepancies between some of the shifts shown by the two measures—as, for example, the sharp upward shift in agricultural employment in North Carolina in the face of practically no change in value of farm products sold—have little connection with the difference in the time period examined. The discrepancies are due, instead, to such factors as the apparent limited gains in the value of labor-intensive activities (dairy products) and the uneven advancement in mechanization among component sectors, as well as other factors peculiar to a specific region which may affect agricultural adjustments within the area. Such discrepancies are themselves of interest in highlighting the interregional changes that have taken place.

per cent of the net upward shift in the value measure shares took place in states that also experienced upward shifts in shares of agricultural employment.

By breaking down the shifts into slow-growth and rapid-growth sectors one can see something of how the changes in value occurred between 1940 and 1954. The shares of the Northeastern states, for example, declined because the slower-growth sectors of agriculture – the dairy products, poultry products, farm forest products, vegetables, and horticultural specialties identified in Table 18 – are concentrated in the highly populous market centers of the Northeast. The dominant dairy states, in particular, reflect the effects of specialization in a slow-growth industry. Texas, Mississippi, and Arkansas, on the other hand, specializing in the rapid-growth sectors – field crops, livestock and products, and fruits and nuts – experienced net upward shifts.

The reasons why some sectors of agriculture have expanded more than others is attributable to a combination of factors. Fruits and nuts and livestock products, for example, tend to have a relatively

Figure 12
Percentage Distribution of Net Shifts in Agricultural Employment, 1939-1958

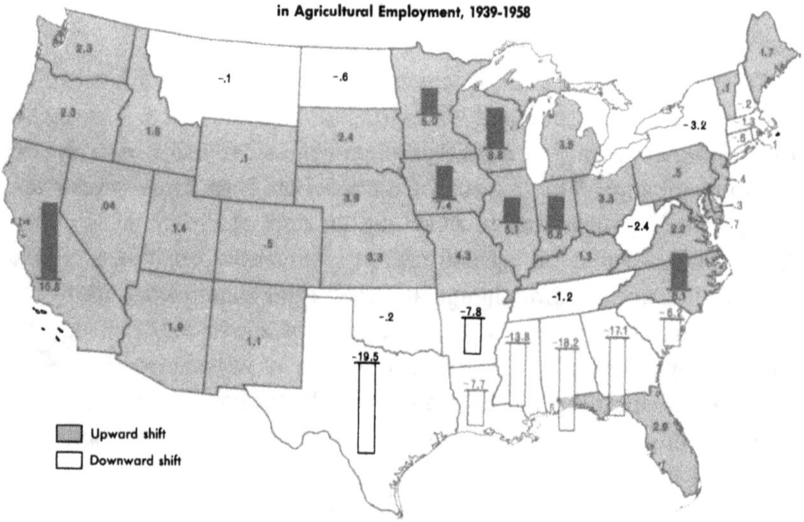

Figure 13
Percentage Distribution of Net Shifts in Value of All Agricultural Products Sold 1940-1954

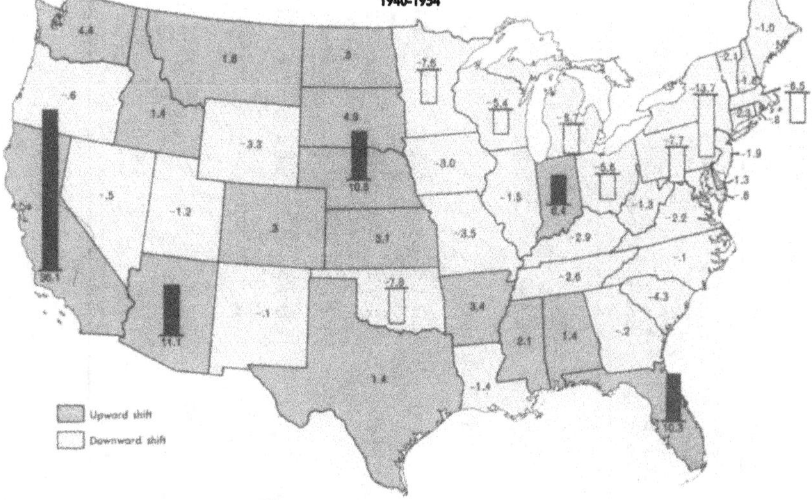

high income elasticity of demand. The substitution of vegetable oils for dairy products, especially noticeable since the repeal of restrictive legislation on oleomargarine, has depressed the position of dairy products in relation to that of field crops. A similar effect has resulted from mechanization, which is capable of greater application to field crops than to dairying. Farm price supports, more often extended to storable commodities than to others, may also have contributed to the rapid-growth characteristics of field crops. And the acreage restrictions associated with price supports may have spurred increased use of chemical fertilizer to bring about increased yields.

Advancing agricultural technology associated with soybeans, hybrid corn, drought-resistant wheats, new feed sorghums, and cotton have all combined to generate a shift in these field crop activities into the western states. The same is generally true of livestock products. The Southeast experienced some gain from an over-all expansion of certain of these products. However, since this shift into the Southeast was part of the adjustment away from labor-intensive row-cropping, it was consistent with – and indeed, contributed to – the downward shift in farm employment in this region.

Table 18. Relative importance of net shifts in value of agricultural product sold, 1940-1954

2-Digit agricultural categories	Value of agricultural products sold				Absolute change 1940-54 (million dollars)	Percentage increase (Col. 5 as per cent of Col. 1)	Total Net shift 1940-54 (million dollars)	Net shift as per cent of:	
	1940		1954						
	(Million dollars)	Per cent	(Million dollars)	Per cent				Absolute Change	1940 value
	(1)	(2)	(3)	(4)	(5)	(6)	(7)	(8)	(9)
All agricultural products sold	6,682	100.0	24,642	100.0	17,960	268.8	± 1,649.2	± 9.2	± 24.7
Field crops	2,471	37.0	9,922	40.3	7,451	301.6	± 1,204.9	± 16.2	± 48.8
Vegetables	200	3.0	645	2.6	446	223.3	± 122.7	± 27.5	± 61.4
Fruits and nuts	295	4.4	1,199	4.9	903	305.8	± 146.3	± 16.2	± 49.6
Horticultural specialties	129	1.9	454	1.8	324	250.8	± 53.1	± 16.4	± 41.2
Dairy products	1,118	16.7	3,334	13.5	2,216	198.2	± 260.8	± 11.8	± 23.3
Poultry and products	555	8.3	1,917	7.8	1,361	245.1	± 324.6	± 23.8	± 58.5
Livestock and products	1,874	28.1	7,041	28.6	5,167	275.7	± 778.5	± 15.1	± 41.5
Farm forest products	39	.6	130	.5	91	233.1	± 33.3	± 36.6	± 85.4

Each region's access to inputs and markets for its agricultural products was modified by many influences. Changes in technology, modifying the land resource requirements, have resulted in shifts based upon the new requirements. The introduction of mechanical cotton pickers, for instance, has brought about a change-over from the cultivation of small fields, often with uneven terrain, to large relatively level tracts of land; hence, the shift of cotton out of the South to the Southwest. Soil exhaustion has been an important factor, as have competing prices for land which result in shifts in land use from one kind of agricultural activity to another or to urban use. By altering the competitive conditions of land use, changes in one production system have altered the location and character of otherwise independent production systems. These general causative factors help to explain the influence of agriculture upon the changes shown by the 1939-58 shifts in employment among individual states (see Figure 7).

The Effects of Agriculture on Employment in Specific Regions

The Areas of Relative Employment Growth

Agriculture contributed significantly to the increasing shares of total employment in California and Arizona between 1939 and 1958. California claimed nearly 17 per cent of the nation's net upward shift in agricultural employment (see Figure 12) and, for the period 1940-54, 36 per cent of the upward shift in the value of farm products sold (see Figure 13). In the various sectors of agricultural activity, during this shorter period, California's share in the upward shifts in terms of agricultural products sold was as follows: field crops – 22 per cent; fruits and nuts – 12 per cent; vegetables – 57 per cent; dairy products – 25 per cent; poultry products – 15 per cent; and livestock products – 12 per cent.

These changes have been associated with important changes in access conditions. An expanding local market has stimulated the production of meat, poultry, and dairy products and, to a lesser degree, of vegetables. Increasing national demand for these products has resulted in increased shipments of California products to the East. But many of the changes cannot be explained solely on grounds of evolving markets. Innovations in mechanization and irrigation have significantly influenced developments in cotton production. Improvements in transportation, storage, and processing of fruits, vegetables, and horticultural specialties have greatly increased the importance of California's resources for producing such products.

Arizona's experience has been similar to California's. If anything, considering its smaller size, this state has benefited to an even greater extent from its agricultural growth.

The area that includes Texas and extends up through the mid-Mountain states is, generally, an economic growth area. In this area, however, the influence of agriculture has tended to run counter to the growth performance of the region. Between 1940 and 1954, Wyoming and Nevada showed very little relative strength in any sector of agriculture. Utah, oriented to the expanding West Coast market, showed some strength in dairying, but in little else. Colorado made some gains in livestock. Texas and New Mexico gained in field crops, but Texas was weak in practically every other sector.

All of these states experienced relative losses or only marginal gains in the value of farm products sold, and all, except Colorado, Utah, and New Mexico, showed relative employment losses or very marginal gains. In terms of agricultural employment, the downward shift for Texas was marked enough to be an important counter to the state's over-all employment growth trend.

Florida, a major growth state, claimed over 10 per cent of the total net upward shift in the value of farm products sold, experiencing an upward shift in every farm sector. This included 58 per cent of the total shift for fruits and nuts, 11 per cent of the total in vegetables, and 7 per cent of the total in dairy products. Yet in spite of these substantial relative gains, Florida's upward shifts in agricultural employment accounted for only 4.8 per cent of its relative gains in all employment.

Of the states in the Great Lakes region showing relative growth, only Indiana significantly improved its standing through agriculture. Some 47 per cent of its shift in total employment came from a net upward shift in agricultural employment. This seems to grow out of favorable input attributes in relation to the corn-soy-hog culture, a sector which has been affected by important innovations.

The Areas of Relative Employment Decline

All the major areas of relative decline in shares of the nation's total employment were affected by their declining shares of agricultural activities. In the Deep South, downward shifts in agricultural employment between 1939 and 1958 accounted for 63 per cent of the total employment shift in Alabama, 59 per cent in Arkansas, 52 per cent in Georgia, 64 per cent in Mississippi, and 56 per cent in South Carolina. These states had sizable downward shifts in field crops, vegetables, and fruits. Upward shifts in meat, poultry, dairy products, and forest products brought about some upward shifts in the value of farm products, but in employment terms these activities did not begin to offset the labor-intensive forms of farm employment they replaced.

Most of the Lakes, Plains, and northern Mountain states showed upward shifts in their share of agricultural employment, supported for the most part by relative gains in field crops and livestock. In the case of Wisconsin, dairy products were large contributors, and in Minnesota vegetables and eggs were major factors. However, these upward shifts were only *relative* within an over-all declining rate of national agricultural employment. These states, being agricultural specialists, received the full impact of the over-all effect generated by a declining industry.

In the Appalachian states the downward shifts in total employment were dominated by other sectors of the economy, particularly mining. Except for West Virginia, which had an adjustment much like that in the Deep South, agriculture contributed little to the net shifts in total employment experienced by any of these states.

The behavior of each of the chief components of agriculture is examined in the original study on which this book is based. Some of the conclusions reached have been used here in surveying the shifts shown among the states. In this shorter version the livestock products sector is selected for emphasis because, together with field crops, it has substantially influenced the changes shown in total agricultural employment.

Livestock Products

Livestock products constitute the second most important sector of the agricultural economy. In 1954, when field crops, the largest sector in terms of value, accounted for 40 per cent of the total value of farm products sold, livestock products claimed almost 29 per cent.

Between 1940 and 1954, the value of livestock products sold increased by more than the average for all farm products. Thus, the states specializing in their production – the Mountain and Plains states and some of the Great Lakes states – had a "composition" gain on this score.

Over 50 per cent of the inputs of the livestock products sector come from agriculture, particularly feed grains and forage. Access to high-quality land resources is not directly important as it is for field crops, but access to the feed sectors tends to be an important locational determinant (unless offset by an unusually strong market pull). Less than 10 per cent of the meat output goes to final demand; 81 per cent goes to intermediate processors, chiefly packing houses. Since this intermediate processing involves considerable weight loss, the tendency is for the packing houses to locate near the livestock sources, thus increasing the significance of access to basic feed inputs. Even though livestock products are relatively expensive to transport, either dressed or on the hoof, this has not counterbalanced the importance of feed inputs and the weight-loss characteristic of intermediate pro-

Figure 14
Percentage Distribution of Net Shifts in Value of Livestock Products Sold, 1940-1954

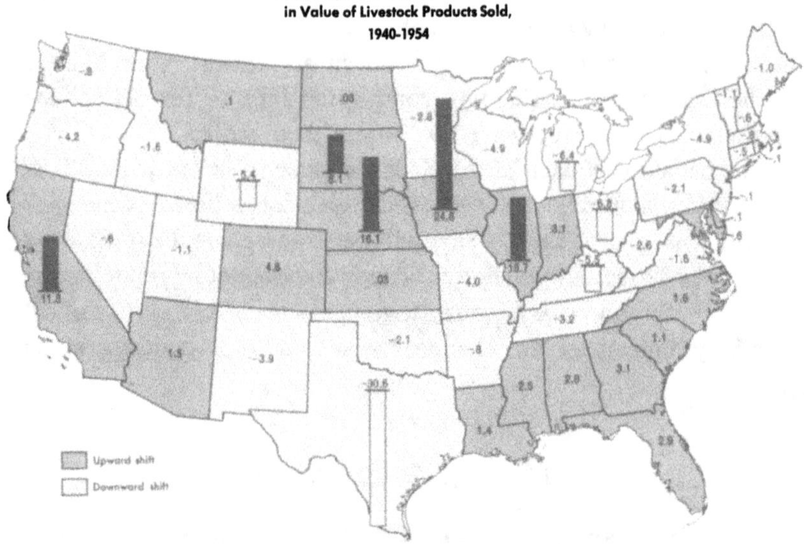

cessing. But it has been a sufficiently important factor to bring about some degree of regional specialization in feeder-stock and finish-feeding with finish-feeding done as close as possible to the source of high-grade finishing feeds and to the packers.

The major upward shifts shown in Figure 14 were in the Corn Belt states, California, and the Southeast. Access to feed is certainly the dominant factor behind the largest net upward shifts – those in the corn-soy belt. Before 1940, hybrid corn was influential in expanding the productivity of this region; and the increasing practice of finish-feeding together with a phenomenal increase in the use of chemical fertilizers has continued the expansion.

The Southeast's upward shift is similarly associated with a relative increase in its access to feed sources. This is part of the story of adjustment away from the row-cropping systems that have debilitated the soil of this region. Rational adjustments in the Southeast call for an extension of cover-cropping, and this expansion of potential livestock feed encourages an expansion of livestock activities. Technology has aided this shift by introducing new pesticides and experimenting with strains of stock (the Brahmin, for instance, and Red Sindi crossed with Jersey) that are adapted to warmer climates. The adjustment is slow, however, because of the relatively heavy capital investments required and because intermediate processing units are not as readily available in the Southeast as in areas of established livestock activity. It is also restrained by the outmoded institutional factors inherent in the region's historical development. Handling livestock successfully calls for new skills, particularly managerial ability. Nevertheless, a definite adjustment seems to be under way.

Most of the Southwestern and Mountain states display net downward shifts in value of livestock products sold. These states are livestock specialists but they appear to have suffered relative losses in input access for several reasons: (1) They are predominantly feeder-stock areas; consequently the increased practice of finish-feeding downgrades their standing when growth is measured in terms of agricultural value. (2) Much of the mid-Mountain region has been overgrazed, leading to a deterioration in access to feeds in some sections. (3) Competitive land uses may have occasioned some loss of access to feeds in Texas and New Mexico. Cotton and grain sorghums, for example, have made striking gains in acreage in these states. (4) Prolonged periods of drought in some areas during the late forties and early fifties have also taken their toll of output and farm sales.

The significant upward shift in California is of particular interest because it reflects a large increase in the regional market. The remoteness of the Far West region tends to place it outside the dominant national transfer patterns for livestock products; consequently the regional market exerts a stronger modifying influence than is usual for the nation as a whole.

In general, then, it can be seen how intricate and interrelated are the forces that bring about interregional shifts in the production of a given farm product. Feeds, soil conditions, changing transportation costs, new processing arrangements, competitive land uses, and changing market sizes — all these and other factors come into play to bring about continual shifts in relative position. This also suggests the many things that require attention if a region consciously sets out to improve its relative position with regard to a generally attractive type of farming.

8. Changes in Manufacturing Employment

In 1958, manufacturing, a large and dynamic sector of the national economy, provided work for 28 per cent of the nation's total labor force, as compared with 13 per cent for all of the resource categories (agriculture, mining, forestry, and fisheries). Only the fast-growing services sector exceed it in volume of employment. In explaining shifts in total employment the role of manufacturing is especially important because it is the basic link between the resource sectors and consuming sectors of the economy and therefore is exposed to sources of change on both sides. Shifts in manufacturing employment accounted for over a third of the total net shift in employment between 1939 and 1958. The net shift in manufacturing employment between 1939 and 1958 represented 18.6 per cent of all manufacturing employment in 1939 and 9.4 per cent of all manufacturing employment in 1958.

Determinants of Location

Except for the agricultural output that is recycled into agriculture, manufacturing uses the largest share of inputs coming from resource sectors. However, it does not necessarily follow that resources have been dominant in shaping structure and change in the manufacturing sector. In manufacturing, from the first resource-processing stage through successive, weight-losing stages, production becomes increasingly freed from its resource base to seek larger concentrations of population which can provide more strategic market locations. For all stages of manufacturing, taken in broad categories, closeness to market tends to be the dominant locational factor. That there are exceptions in specific cases goes without saying as, for example, in the part that oil and gas has played in the growth of manufacturing in the Southwest.

Another determinant influencing the location of manufacturing industries is their need of inputs from within manufacturing itself. Almost 40 per cent of manufacturing output is absorbed in this way. Consequently, a large part of manufacturing activity is dependent upon intra-industry links for both inputs and outputs and must seek locations where intermediate markets and sources of supply are within relatively easy reach. (The extent to which many of the manufacturing industries exchange their products in the process of manufacture is shown in Table 19.) A clustering of activities is likely to result, which usually leads to greater degrees of industrial specialization generating economies in which all can share. Thus evolve the great urban-metropolitan regions with interrelated sets of consumption, service, and manufacturing activities which over time develop magnet-like attributes.

Table 19. Per cent of inputs coming from manufacturing and per cent of outputs going to manufacturing for selected 2-digit manufacturing categories, 1947

2-Digit manufacturing categories	Per cent of inputs	Per cent of outputs
Food products	25.4	18.8
Textiles	24.5	*70.2*
Apparel	*44.2*	18.3
Wood and paper products	38.4	*47.0*
Chemicals	*43.0*	*60.6*
Petroleum products	13.1	20.8
Coke and coal products	20.2	*56.7*
Rubber products	*45.5*	*41.9*
Glass and other nonmetals	23.0	*42.4*
Primary metals	*46.0*	*84.0*
Secondary metals	*47.4*	*89.7*
Metal fabricating	*48.8*	*44.4*
Machinery	*44.2*	36.2
Electrical apparatus	*44.9*	36.6
Transportation equipment	*62.5*	24.8
Miscellaneous manufacturing	*42.2*	24.4
National average for all manufacturing	39.4	39.4

Note: Figures in italics are above the average

The westward movement of population and economic growth, a strong characteristic of the 1939-58 period, has brought about interregional shifts in final markets which, in turn, have influenced the location of intermediate markets. This has had some adverse effects upon the Manufacturing Belt's relative access to markets, and these are particularly noticeable in the eastern end of the Belt. With expanding regional markets associated with the "filling-in" process of regional growth, areas outside the Manufacturing Belt appear to be taking over some of the locational advantages hitherto held by areas within the Belt. California's great growth in manufacturing, for example, is partly the product of cumulative expansion through which important intermediate supply and market functions have made feasible some operations which formerly were not economic. Changes in transportation costs have been a factor in the interregional shifts. The relative decline in the cost of short overland hauls and of small lots, compared with that of long hauls and large lots, has helped the Southeast and West to increase their shares of manufacturing.

Effects of Interregional Shifts

The interregional movements in total employment have been greatly affected by the shifts in manufacturing production worker employment, shown in Figure 15.[1] Most extreme are the effects shown in California, with 45 per cent of the net upward shifts in manufacturing, and in Texas, where the net upward shift is 15 per cent of the total upward shifts. Wisconsin and a group of states in the Plains and the Southeast show gains in manufacturing in spite of relative losses in population and total employment. These states are characterized by resource specialization and/or population pressure, and therefore attract manufacturing processes oriented more to labor and resource inputs than to markets.

[1]It should be noted that the manufacturing activities examined in this chapter are based on "manufacturing production worker employment." This is because accurate total employment figures are not available at the 2-digit industry level. This change in measure represents a difference of 1.2 million manufacturing workers in 1939 and 0.6 million in 1958, which is insignificant when distributed among the states in terms of relative shifts. It should be borne in mind, also, that the shifts represent only a small part of the absolute changes in manufacturing employment. The net shift in manufacturing production worker employment was only 14 per cent of total manufacturing employment in 1939 and 21 per cent of the increase in such employment between 1939 and 1958. Nevertheless, because of the large volume of manufacturing employment the shifts have a significant impact on state employment. They also have an important multiplier effect on service employment. For a comparison with the shifts for total employment, see Chapter 5, especially Table 9.

Figure 15
Percentage Distribution of Net Shifts
in Total Manufacturing Production Worker
Employment, 1939-1958

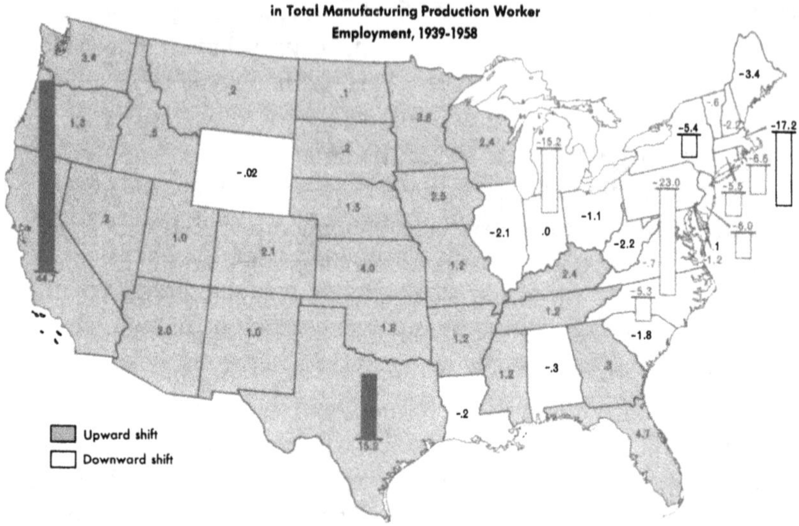

Most of the net downward shift in manufacturing is distributed through New England, the Great Lakes, and Middle Atlantic. But in seven of the twelve manufacturing specialist states, the downward shift is only relative. While they did not experience growth rates commensurate with their expected growth (measured against the national rate), their manufacturing employment did grow in absolute terms. The trend of absolute manufacturing growth for these regions is shown in Table 3.

The over-all effect of the changes in manufacturing has been to produce a moderate relative shift out of the Manufacturing Belt into the Southeast, Southwest, and Far West; but the shift would have been more marked were it not for the fact that the Manufacturing Belt states specialize heavily in rapid-growth manufacturing sectors–those that are growing at a faster rate than the national average. What has been happening in the Belt states is illustrated by Figures 16 and 17, which show a marked downward shift in the local-factor effect in contrast to a marked upward shift in the composition effect engendered by rapid-growth specialization. As noted in Chapter 5, the nature of this type of measurement makes it impossible to compare the two figures directly. However, they are useful not only in classifying the behavior of manufacturing in the Belt states, but in providing

Figure 16
Percentage Distribution of Local-Factor Net Shifts in All Manufacturing Production Worker Employment, 1939-1958

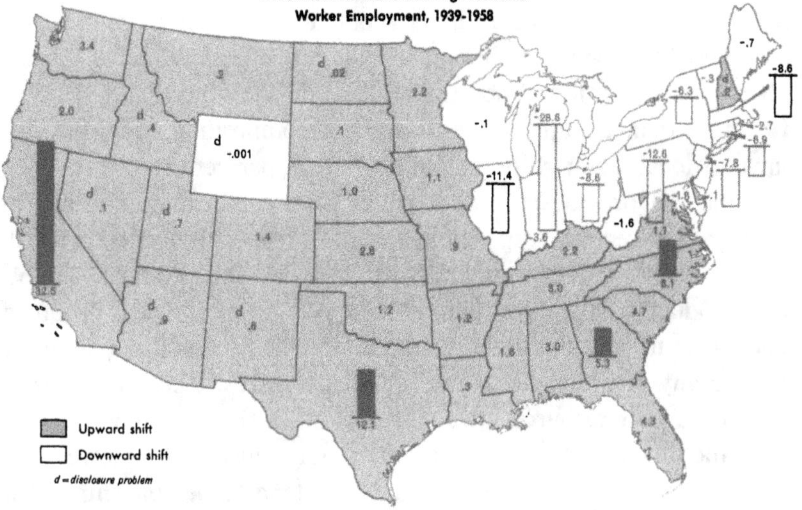

Figure 17
Percentage Distribution of Composition Net Shift in All Manufacturing Production Worker Employment, 1939-1958

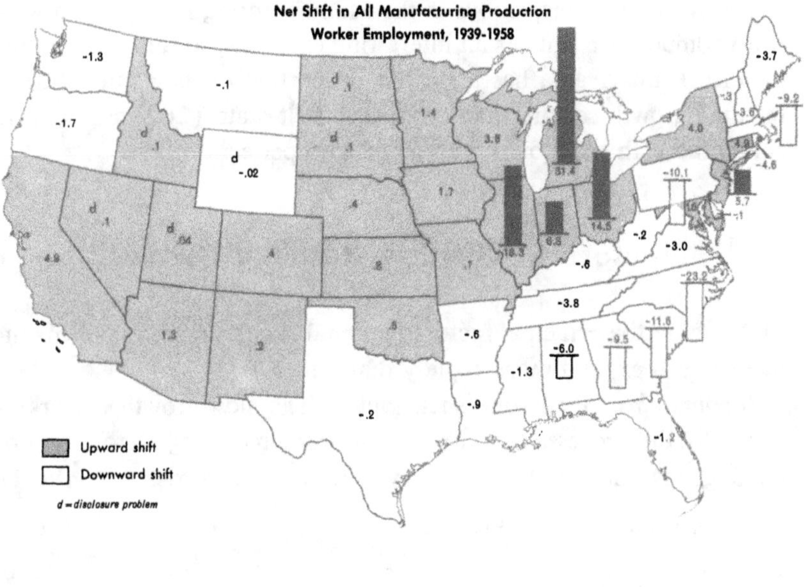

an important key to understanding regional differentials in the United States.[2] The net upward composition shift has been significant in volume terms only in the Manufacturing Belt and California. Michigan, Illinois, Ohio, and Indiana account for 71 per cent, but their share of the downward shift in local-factor effects amounts to only 53 per cent. North and South Carolina, on the other hand, account for more than a third of the downward composition shift, but had upward local-factor shifts amounting to 13 per cent.

Table 20 provides the data behind the composition shifts. The slow-growth sectors responsible for the composition effect (textile mill products, tobacco manufactures, leather and products, lumber and products, apparel, primary metals, petroleum and coal products, and furniture and fixtures) are made up chiefly of soft goods industries, many of which receive an important part of their inputs from the primary or resource-extracting sectors of the economy. In addition, the slow-growth sectors are often more sensitive to interregional differences in the cost of labor, and they tend to be concentrated in the states outside the Manufacturing Belt. The rapid-growth sectors are predominantly hard goods industries. Their ties are less close to the resource sectors and they are concentrated in the Manufacturing Belt states plus Iowa, Minnesota, Arizona, and California. The case of Pennsylvania, conspicuous in the Manufacturing Belt for its downward composition shift, is an interesting exception to this distribution pattern. Pennsylvania has a smaller proportion of its manufacturing in rapid-growth sectors than any other Belt state (26.9 per cent as compared with a national average of 35.6 per cent in 1939).

Factors Governing Rates of Growth

What are the principal factors that enable certain sectors of manufacturing to expand more rapidly than others?

Income elasticity is one such factor. The slow-growth sectors — generally the processed food and basic resource-using sectors — produce goods for which demand varies little with rising consumer

[2]In many instances the disclosure rule adhered to by the Census prevents basic manufacturing data from becoming available. As a consequence, the percentage figures recorded for each state in Figures 16 and 17 are approximations only. A "d" indicates a state for which the disclosure problem is especially acute; here the percentage has been estimated on an average, across-the-board basis. In each case, however, at least the direction of the shifts is unlikely to be subject to error.

Table 20. Relative importance of net employment shifts in manufacturing production workers, 1939-58

2-Digit manufacturing categories	Manufacturing production worker employment				Absolute change 1939-58	Percentage increase (Col. 5 as per cent of Col. 1)	Total net shift 1939-58	Net shift as per cent of:	
	1939	Per cent	1958	Per cent				Absolute change	1939 employment
	(1)	(2)	(3)	(4)	(5)	(6)	(7)	(8)	(9)
Total manufacturing production workers	7,808,205	100.0	15,489,938	100.0	7,681,733	98.4	± 1,450,230	± 18.9	± 18.6
Electrical machinery	247,930	3.2	1,010,222	6.5	762,292	307.5	± 171,487	± 22.5	± 69.2
Instruments and related products	84,867	1.1	282,986	1.8	198,119	233.4	± 48,665	± 24.6	± 57.3
Transportation equipment	544,553	7.0	1,624,992	10.5	1,080,439	198.4	± 592,368	± 54.8	± 108.8
Machinery (exc. electrical)	536,082	6.9	1,551,587	10.0	1,015,505	189.4	± 180,313	± 17.8	± 33.6
Chemicals and allied products	275,669	3.5	741,150	4.8	465,481	168.9	± 107,449	± 23.1	± 39.0
Printing and publishing	324,371	4.2	860,781	5.6	536,410	165.4	± 69,374	± 12.9	± 21.4
Miscellaneous manufacturing	241,725	3.1	617,141	4.0	375,416	155.3	± 100,349	± 26.7	± 41.5
Fabricated metal products	451,087	5.8	1,037,627	6.7	586,540	130.1	± 121,343	± 20.7	± 26.9
Food and kindred products	802,133	10.3	1,683,822	10.9	881,689	109.9	± 148,743	± 16.9	± 18.5
Stone, clay, and glass products	267,094	3.4	558,612	3.6	291,518	109.1	± 78,652	± 27.0	± 29.4
Paper and allied products	270,239	3.5	555,224	3.6	284,985	105.5	± 70,584	± 24.8	± 26.1
Rubber products	120,740	1.5	230,832	1.5	110,092	91.2	± 24,902	± 22.6	± 20.6
Furniture and fixtures	189,382	2.4	359,520	2.3	170,138	89.8	± 47,939	± 28.2	± 25.3
Petroleum and coal products	107,695	1.4	182,687	1.2	74,992	69.6	± 34,970	± 46.6	± 32.5
Primary metal industry	672,438	8.6	1,071,675	6.9	399,237	59.4	± 110,387	± 27.6	± 16.4
Apparel and related products	752,829	9.6	1,182,103	7.6	429,274	57.0	± 186,239	± 43.4	± 24.7
Lumber and products	422,947	5.4	579,936	3.7	156,989	37.1	± 76,582	± 48.8	± 18.1
Leather and leather products	327,189	4.2	347,472	2.2	20,283	6.2	± 29,920	± 147.5	± 9.1
Tobacco manufactures	87,525	1.1	88,063	.6	538	.6	± 21,720	± 4,037.2	± 24.8
Textile mill products	1,081,710	13.8	923,506	6.0	— 158,204	— 14.5	± 159,335	± 100.7	± 14.7

Note: Detailed state data are scanty in several 2-digit categories because they have been withheld for disclosure reasons. Because of this, total upward and total downward net shifts can vary widely. The means are shown in Col. 7.

income compared with the more highly fabricated products of manufacturing activity. The only rapid-growth sectors that can be classed as resource-using (rubber, paper, and chemicals) are those whose products are most likely to enjoy increasing demand because they supply intermediate necessities for the most rapidly growing industries in the economy.

Sector substitution is another important part of the explanation in many cases. One of the reasons why forest products industries are in the slow-growth group is that substitutions of metals and plastics have transferred some production jobs from these to other manufacturing sectors.

Exports of the more highly finished manufactured goods have gained relatively over such goods as food, textiles, and apparel in the manufacturing export total, just as the manufacturing sector as a whole has tended to gain a larger share of the nation's exports relative to the resource sectors.

Gains in labor productivity have been greater in some manufacturing sectors than in others. For example, the substantial decline in employment in tobacco manufactures arises from the fact that this industry, in the face of inelastic demand, made one of the greatest increases in wage-earner efficiency. When the employment measure is used, advances in mechanization and similar improvements have a deflating effect on the measure, decreasing the rate of growth of the rapid-growth industries, and accentuating the increases in growth of the slow-growth industries. In general, the industries classed here as rapid-growth industries have made the greatest gains in labor productivity.

Changes in the composition of the consuming sectors of the economy have been important. During the 1939-58 period, the government absorbed a much larger share of the output than formerly – particularly in the area of military defense. The sectors most apt to benefit from this shift in demand composition are those producing such products as electrical machinery, transport equipment, and so on. Other changes in consumption demand have arisen from the rising rate of new household formation.

These factors suggest the types of influences at work in generating the kinds of growth that have determined the composition effects in manufacturing employment.

To understand the behavior of the local-factor shifts, it is necessary to trace the patterns of development in each of the twenty 2-digit sectors of manufacturing employment, on which the shift measurements are based. Detailed analysis of the changes in each component is presented in the comprehensive study from which this shorter version is adapted. Here, however, examination must be confined to two highly significant sectors of manufacturing employment – metal products and chemical products – that illustrate some of the facets of the internal structure of manufacturing and some of the regional changes that have occurred.

Metal Products

The metal products sector of the economy, together with primary metals, are closely tied together through intra-industry relationships on both the input and output side of the market. These are the industries that have built up the highest concentrations in the Manufacturing Belt. They find their best location orientation within an agglomerated complex of activities (a) because of the important intra-industry ties, (b) because of the important external economies that attend clustering and specialization in an urban metropolitan complex, and (c) because these are often industries for which internal scale economies are important, and which are oriented more to national markets than to regional markets.

The metal products industries – fabricated metal products, electrical and nonelectrical machinery, and transportation equipment – constitute, separately, some of the largest and most dynamic sectors of the U. S. manufacturing economy. When they are combined they account for one-third of all manufacturing employment. Their interstate shifts between 1939 and 1958, seen in Figure 18, amounted to almost 50 per cent of their total combined 1939 employment. In transportation equipment, the shift equaled 109 per cent of the total 1939 employment in that sector.

Except for New Jersey, Connecticut, and California, the outstanding states in these rapid-growth sectors are all concentrated in the western end of the Manufacturing Belt. It follows that over 80 per cent of the net upward composition shift in total manufacturing employment is also concentrated here (see Figure 17). However, with decentralized production in some of the categories, such as trans-

Figure 18
Percentage Distribution of Net Shifts
in Metal Products Industries Employment
1939-1958

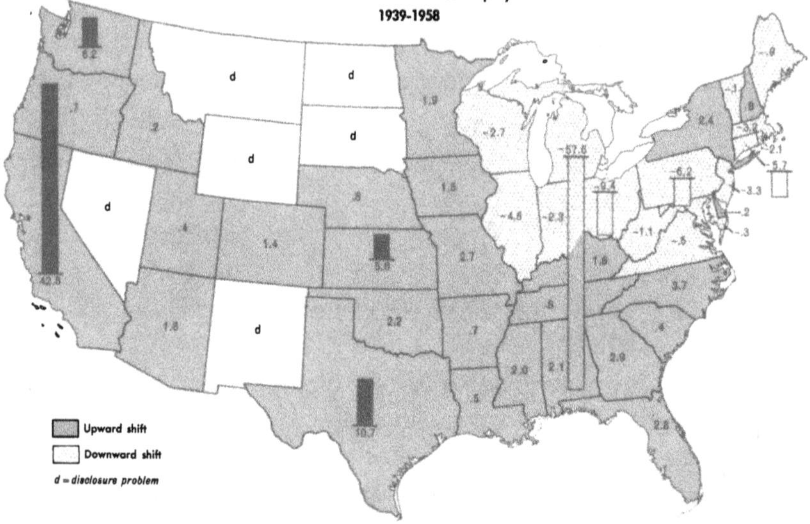

portation equipment, the effects of the local-factor shifts have been dominant and the western end of the Manufacturing Belt has lost relative standing in the metal products industries as a whole. Basically, with the exception of New York, the shift is out of the Belt states and into the Southeast and West, with California experiencing the major gains and Michigan the major (relative) losses. The general configuration of these shifts closely corresponds to the local-factor shift in manufacturing employment shown in Figure 16. This is a key element in explaining the total shift picture.

What major factors lead to these extensive shifts?

Contrary to what is often assumed, regional changes in access to primary metal inputs have had relatively little effect on the shifts in the metal products industries. The reverse, in fact, is probable since, under modern technology, iron and steel products and all forms of metal rolling and drawing – the major part of primary metals activity – tend to be market-oriented. Since these industries usually sell to agglomerated markets, it is probable that the shifts in the metal products industries are partly a result of shifts in the markets they serve and partly are caused by regional changes in the agglomeration economies they find so significant. Discussion of the characteristic shifts taking place within a few of the key 3-digit components of the metal products industry may help to explain the way in which these dual influences can work.

First, let us look at some of the industry groups for which agglomeration is not apparently essential: tin can production, mining machinery production, the structural metals industry, the ships and boats industry, and the aircraft industry. Together, these five industry groups account for between 15 and 20 per cent of the total employment in the metal-fabricating group. All are oriented either to final markets or to intermediate markets or to inputs that are not tied in with the agglomerations of the Manufacturing Belt.

The production of tin cans is strongly oriented to the production of food products, their particular market. The low-value product acquires great bulk in processing, and therefore the industry has located near major food-processing plants – often to the extent of being connected by a common conveyor. The shift pattern shows that the regions making the greatest gain (California, Florida, and some of the Plains states) also have made the greatest gains in the production of food products subject to canning.

The production of mining machinery also seems to be market-oriented – and, again, to an essentially resource market. For example, Texas produces almost half of the oil-mining machinery, with California and Oklahoma the runners-up. The Southwest shows the principal upward shifts here. This industry produces a highly specialized product and, consequently, sells important services as well as machinery. Therefore, close communication with the market is important.

The structural metal products industry and the ships and boats industry appear to be oriented to final markets or to intermediate markets closely associated with final markets. Only slightly more than half of the former group's production is in the Manufacturing Belt. Agglomeration economies seem less important, in part because most of its inputs come from primary and secondary metal groups. Its shift pattern is predominately into the Southeast and West, following the more general shifts in construction employment and its association with shifting final and intermediate markets. The ships and boats industry has displayed marked downward shifts from the Middle Atlantic region into the Great Lakes states, the Gulf states, and the Pacific Coast states. This is largely due to an unprecedented boom in the construction of small pleasure craft.

The aircraft industry has been the most dynamic sector in the metal products group. Its growth rate was over 1,000 per cent for the period 1939-54. The engine and propeller segments of the industry have tended to stay concentrated in the Manufacturing Belt, but airframes and finished aircraft production has displayed rather remarkable mobility. As early as 1940 one-half of the industry's capacity had moved from its original location. Inputs are widespread in source, high in value, and easily shipped. The industry started in the East with New York City as a center. It moved to the West Coast – partly in response to labor supplies that were actually and potentially available, partly because of a climate suited for testing planes and to outside work (as well as permitting less expensive buildings), and partly because surplus government buildings were available. Recently the industry apparently has been shifting eastward again, with Texas, Oklahoma, Kansas, Georgia, and Alabama all showing important expansions. The increasing use of jet planes in civilian aircraft is likely to influence the location decisions of the aircraft industry, since noise and the danger associated with test flights place constraints on testing jets over populated areas.

The movements of these five sectors, all concentrated in areas outside the Manufacturing Belt, go far to explain the shifts shown in Figure 18.

A second group consists of industries which traditionally have been partially tied to agglomeration economies, but currently are showing significant shifts out of the Manufacturing Belt. Examples are the automobile industry, the agricultural machinery and tractor industry, service and household machinery, and communication equipment.

One reason for the outward shifts may be that two attributes of the Manufacturing Belt – the large-scale operations necessary to economical production in the metal-fabricating industry, and proximity to a variety of intermediate suppliers and markets – have to a degree become available elsewhere in recent years. Regions like the Far West have become more diversified, enabling them to serve as loci for economical production.

Another reason may be found in the diseconomies that can accompany the economies of well-established areas of agglomeration. Rising labor costs in the Manufacturing Belt and rising transportation costs, for example, may be offsetting some of the advantages of the region for these industries.

The automobile industry has almost three-quarters of its employment in three states – Michigan, Ohio, and Indiana. Michigan alone accounts for over half of the total. The vast complex of suppliers and service functions which centers on Detroit has proved to be vulnerable, however. Michigan has incurred large relative losses in this industry (over 80 per cent of the net downward shift; in the post-war period the losses have been absolute). To some extent the shift out of Michigan represents a readjustment within the agglomeration complex. The principal gainer was Ohio, but Indiana and Illinois also experienced relative upward shifts. But part of the shift has been to more distant areas. Savings in transport and assembly costs are pulling automobile assembly towards expanding markets. Some 60 per cent of the net upward shift is outside the Great Lakes complex, with such states as California, Kansas, Texas, and Massachusetts making important gains.

Other industries appear to share in this trend toward decentralization. The *agricultural machinery and tractor industry* has displayed a decided shift of production out of Illinois and Wisconsin to areas closer to regional markets. This is largely because a movement is under way to establish branch assembly plants to save on heavy freight costs from the Midwest. *Service and household machinery* and *communication equipment* also show similar influences.

For proper perspective, however, it is important to take note of two things. (1) The operating core of these industries remains in the Manufacturing Belt. The major shifts involve branch assembly plants – that part of the industry's operation that benefits least from agglomeration economies. (2) The major expansion outside the Manufacturing Belt has been concentrated in California, Texas, Kansas, and Georgia, states which are centrally located for access to large multistate market areas. Thus, even in decentralization, agglomeration economies seem to have been instrumental in shaping the location pattern.

For a third group of industries comprising *engines and turbines, insulated cable and wire, engine, electrical equipment, and railroad equipment,* the Manufacturing Belt retains all of its traditional importance. All concentrate close to 100 per cent of their employment there. Indeed, in the case of railroad equipment, the Manufacturing Belt has strengthened its hold; faced with the completion of dieselization and serious competition from other transport, most of the other producing areas have experienced absolute declines in this employment.

Taking the metal products groups as a whole, however, it is evident that the shifts and countershifts of the individual components add up to a trend away from the Manufacturing Belt. In 1939, the four 2-digit metal products sectors – fabricated metal products, electrical machinery, nonelectrical machinery, and transportation equipment – concentrated 87 per cent of their total employment in the Manufacturing Belt; in 1958 this had dropped to 70 per cent. If these changes continue, they could bring about significant changes in the locational structure of American manufacturing, particularly since the industries involved have important input-output ties with other segments of manufacturing activity.

Chemicals and Allied Products

Although the chemical products sector accounts for only 4.6 per cent of manufacturing employment, it has generated important composition and local-factor effects on the total. Its employment shifts among the states between 1939 and 1958 equaled 39 per cent of its 1939 employment. The industry is in a rapid state of change. Between 1939 and 1954 (the last year for which suitable data at the 3-digit industry level were available at the time of analysis), employment in industrial inorganic materials and drugs and medicines increased by almost 150 per cent, and employment in industrial organic chemicals more than doubled. Technology has brought extraordinary advances; Dupont reports that over half of its output represents products that were either unknown or in their commercial infancy in the 1930's.

The net shifts shown in Figure 19 testify to the far-reaching impact of chemical products upon the changing patterns of manufacturing employment. The pronounced gains in Texas and the rest of the Southwest received strong stimulus from both inorganic chemicals and organic chemicals. In the latter area, with its fine petroleum deposits, the petrochemicals dominate. In the case of inorganic acids and salts, access to sulfur and salt has been important, but so also has access to important intermediate markets in the petrochemical industries. In addition, the region (mostly Texas) made gains in the pro-

Figure 19
Percentage Distribution of Net Shifts in Chemicals and Allied Products Employment, 1939-1958

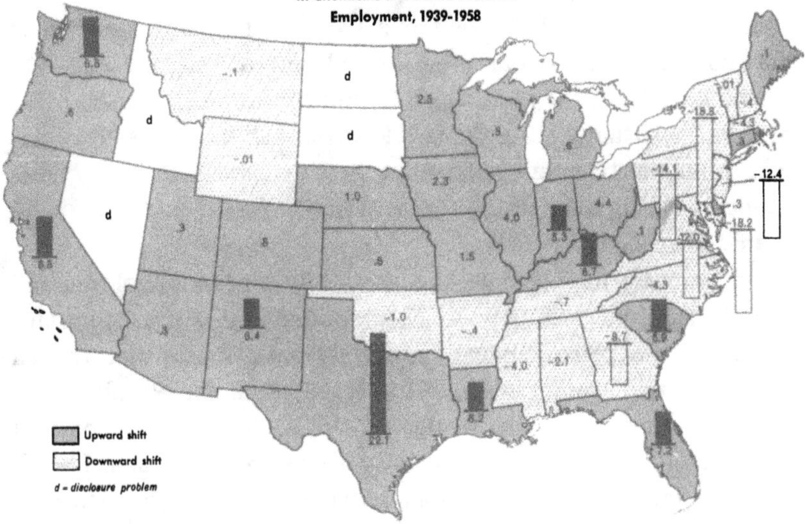

duction of fertilizer and of the more market-oriented soaps and paints.

In the Great Lakes states there was some gain in organic chemicals, primarily plastics, in response to a marked increase in market access combined with the fact that some chemical intermediates can be profitably produced near production markets. There was also some gain in drugs and medicines. But the greatest gains have been in the production of fertilizer and of vegetable and animal oils.

The West Coast's expansion received some stimulus from organic chemicals and vegetable and animal oils. Its major gains, however, have come from those chemical products attracted to expanding markets – drugs, soaps, and paints.

The East lost out in practically every segment except for scattered upward shifts in drugs and medicines, paints, soaps, and miscellaneous chemicals. The Deep South suffered because of heavy downward shifts in fertilizers and in vegetable and animals oils that offset modest upward shifts in other chemicals oriented to its resources and markets.

Obviously, it would be a ponderous task to analyze the behavior of each of the industries included under the umbrella of "chemical products." However, one–industrial organic chemicals–merits mention because its changes in employment typify many that are taking place in other sectors of the total industry.

Industrial Organic Chemicals

Between 1939 and 1954 the Great Lakes and Plains states, Texas and Louisiana, and the Far West showed upward shifts in industrial organic chemicals; the New England and Middle Atlantic states accounted for virtually all of the net downward shifts. The shifts characteristic of plastic intermediates, the most dynamic sector of organic chemicals during the period, are remarkably similar to those for all organic chemicals.

Some sixteen intermediate chemicals based upon petroleum and natural gas alone are used in the production of plastic materials. Studies of the petrochemical industries[3] have found that for all markets in the Southeast and West (other than the Pacific Coast states) production is resource-oriented and would tend to be centered in the major supply areas, particularly Texas and Louisiana. For all markets along the Eastern Seaboard there is a strong tendency to resource orientation, although a few of the chemical intermediates continue to show a tendency to market orientation in this area. Production to serve markets in the Great Lakes and Plains states shows a decidedly mixed tendency. About two-fifths of the processes seem to be resource-oriented and about two-fifths market-oriented; another 20 per cent show no clear-cut cost advantage at either place.

With these generalizations in mind, the regional changes in input-output access can be examined. New England and the Middle Atlantic states have been losing their earlier advantage in access to the intermediate markets. For plastic materials, the latest technology would seem to make it more economical to produce chemical intermediates close to their oil and natural gas sources. Declining access to both total markets and resource inputs in an area that dominated the early production of plastic materials has led to a net downward shift.

The Great Lakes and Plains states made a striking gain in access to markets for plastic materials. But production of plastic materials in these states has not increased correspondingly. For some chemical

[3]Walter Isard and Eugene W. Schooler, *Location Factors in the Petrochemical Industry with Special Reference to Future Expansion in the Arkansas-White-Red River Basins* (Area Development Division, Office of Technical Services, Business and Defense Services, U. S. Department of Commerce, 1955); also Eugene W. Schooler, *Regional Advantage in the Production of Chemicals from Petroleum and Natural Gas*, unpublished doctoral dissertation, Harvard University.

intermediates there is a tendency to market orientation, but for a number of others the petroleum-producing areas are most economic for serving this market.

The Southeast has made a more striking gain in the production of plastic materials than the gain in markets appears to account for. The explanation may be that newer technology has given this region access to important markets for plastics products in other regions. The Pacific area shows an important gain because it has access to an expanding regional market and has its own oil and natural gas sources.

These chemical intermediates that form plastic materials are a good example of mixed location orientation. In some cases the same process can be oriented both to intermediate markets and to resource inputs, depending upon which of several regional markets it is serving.

Two other organic chemicals should be touched upon here. The production of synthetic fibers, basically labor-oriented, has not contributed to the major shifts into the Plains states and the Southwest. Since its major markets are in the textile industry concentrated in the Southeast, where there is also an abundance of cheap labor, 85 per cent of the synthetic fiber production is in this region. On the other hand, the Texas and Louisiana Gulf area has gained a part of its strength from the production of the chemical intermediates that form the synthetic fibers.

Synthetic rubber is another petrochemical that has made a significant contribution to the expansion in organic chemicals in the Southwest. This process appears to be firmly oriented to resource inputs, except for a few of the chemical intermediates that might serve the "Eastern Interior" markets. Consequently, the Manufacturing Belt has been losing employment in the rubber industry; the Southeast and West have claimed all of the recent expansion in the industry and now account for 87 per cent of the total employment.

Possibly more than other industry groups, the industrial organic chemicals category illustrates the complexity of the interregional production shifts that are continually under way. The production of each product has its own particular requirements and over-all regional growth within any given period can only be seen in a realistic light when the changing requirements of at least the major industries are noted. Similarly, analysis of the growth potentials of any region can be meaningful only in the light of its advantages and disadvantages for *specific* economic activities. There is no short-cutting individual industry studies when one wants to understand regional economic growth.

9. Per Capita Income: Levels and Rates of Growth

Regions not only differ in the rates at which their population and volume of economic activities grow, but also differ in their average levels of living and in the rates at which living levels increase. Earlier chapters, especially 1 and 4, demonstrated the extent to which volume and welfare measures can diverge in actual fact. It is important to stress the difference between the changes expressed by the two measures, because they are often confused, particularly in some of the "area development" literature. It is not possible to understand what is taking place in our economy unless the distinction is clearly made, nor is it possible to develop sensible public policy with regard to regional growth unless the differences are appreciated.

The factors that are behind regional differences in average levels of living and in changes in levels of living are discussed in this chapter. But first it is well to look at existing regional patterns. For this the measure used is average per capita income which, while subject to limitations (for example, it fails to indicate how income is distributed in a given area), is still the best over-all measure devised to describe differences in levels of living.

Differences Among the States[1] in Average Per Capita Income

The states and regions tend to group themselves into the three categories of per capita income level shown in Figure 20: (1) the urban-

[1]The sources used here are the state personal income estimates of the U.S. Department of Commerce and the tabulations of family and individual income contained in the 1950 Census reports. The 1960 Census reports on income were not available at the time of writing.

industrialized-service regions of the Manufacturing Belt and the Far West, with per capita incomes above, and mostly well above, the 1959 national average of $2,166; (2) the Mountain, Plains, and Southwest regions, northern New England,[2] and the peripheral southern states of Florida and Virginia, with incomes in a middle range somewhat below the national average; and (3) the greatest part of the Southeast (and the Dakotas) with incomes lower than the 1954 national average of $1,770.

Figure 20
Average State Per Capita Personal Income 1959

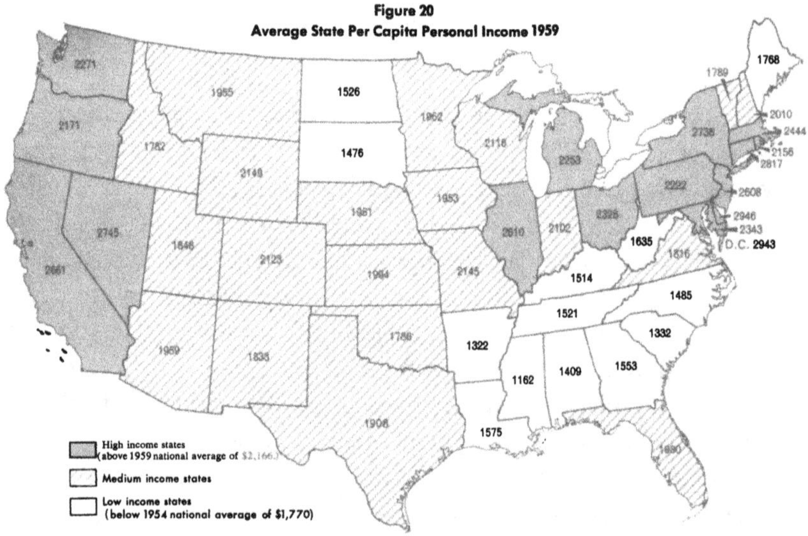

The groupings are fairly well defined. Within the high-income areas, only three states in the Northeast (Indiana, Wisconsin, and Rhode Island) were below the national average in 1959 – and in each case by only a small amount. The per capita income of the low-income states was from $500 to $1,000 below the national average. The middle-income group covered the relatively narrow range between $1,782 (Idaho) and $2,156 (Rhode Island). In terms of regional averages, the range of the estimates is from highs of 18 per cent and 17 per cent *above* the national average for the Far West and the Middle Atlantic, to 28 per cent *below* the national average for the Southeast.

[2] Maine is on the borderline, with an average income just $2.00 below the figure chosen as the dividing line.

Relative variations within the major components of per capita income are of three types:

1. participation income – wages, salaries and other payments for personal services, and proprietors' income;
2. property income – dividends, interest, rent, etc.;
3. transfer payments – pensions, social security payments, etc.

As can be seen from Table 21, property income per capita is the most variable of all income components. Its relative variation among

Table 21. Per capita personal income and its components, by region, selected states, 1959

Region and state[a]	Personal income		Property income		Particiption income	
New England	$2,396		$351		$1,901	
Vermont		$1,789		$247		$1,418
Connecticut		2,817		430		2,274
Middle Atlantic	2,540		368		2,044	
Pennsylvania		2,222		302		1,784
Delaware		2,946		713		2,146
Great Lakes	2,337		285		1,947	
Wisconsin		2,116		267		1,745
Illinois		2,610		327		2,169
Southeast	1,565		173		1,301	
Mississippi		1,162		102		978
Florida		1,980		310		1,542
Plains	1,978		254		1,619	
South Dakota		1,476		200		1,192
Kansas		1,994		273		1,622
Southwest	1,887		230		1,573	
Oklahoma		1,786		216		1,452
Arizona		1,959		199		1,670
Mountain	1,990		253		1,638	
Idaho		1,782		195		1,488
Wyoming		2,149		301		1,775
Far West	2,565		336		2,109	
Oregon		2,171		263		1,795
Nevada		2,745		296		2,376
United States	$2,166		$280		$1,777	
Relative variation[b]	21.2%		39.4%		20.4%	

[a] Regional averages are total personal income for the region divided by population for the region; hence the weighted (by population) average of per capita personal income. In this chapter, Louisiana is treated as part of the Southwest region because of its increasing similarity to other states in the Southwest in industrial structure, particularly as affected by petroleum and natural gas, and therefore in its income structure.

[b] Standard deviation divided by the mean of the state observations.

the states was 39.4 per cent in 1959, or about twice that of participation income. Its level was highest in Delaware ($713) and lowest in Mississippi ($102). In the three highest income regions – the Far West, the Middle Atlantic, and New England – property income per capita was a higher proportion of the total than elsewhere.

Participation income, consisting largely of income from labor services, has amounted on the average to some five-sixths of personal income in recent years.

Net transfer payments amount to about 5 per cent of personal income across the country. (They are not shown in Table 21 but can be calculated by subtracting the figures for per capita property and participation income from personal income.)

Race and Residence

Certain groups in our society tend to receive lower incomes than the bulk of the population no matter where they live or what they do. This is especially true of the Negroes (although it is also true of older persons, physically and mentally handicapped persons, and younger persons with limited education and skill). The income figures for 1949 provided in the 1950 Census show that the median income of rural farm non-whites in the Southeast was $486 compared with $933 for rural farm whites. The differences were almost as substantial in nonfarm sections and in other regions. For example, in the case of urban and rural nonfarm persons in the relatively wealthy Middle Atlantic region, the median income of non-whites was $1,344 compared with $2,330 for whites.

Differences between white and non-white incomes remain substantial even when age, sex, educational, and occupational differences are taken into account. In part, the low-income problem of the Negroes is related to their difficulties in getting and holding jobs. This is illustrated by Labor Department data on unemployment at the end of 1959. Of the number of workers who had been jobless for more than twenty-six weeks, one out of four was non-white, at a time when the ratio of non-whites in the labor force as a whole was one to ten.

Incomes vary directly with the size of place in which the worker lives. The 1949 Census data indicate that higher levels are generally found in the larger cities and also that income *differentials* are greater among small cities than among larger cities. To illustrate, in the Southeastern states in 1949, incomes for white males living in cities of over 500,000 population averaged only 10 per cent below those applying to similar size cities in the Lake states. In cities of 100,000 to 250,000 population, however, the difference was almost 17 per cent. It seems probable, then, that on the whole our larger cities offer more equal opportunities than do smaller cities, but this theory cannot be tested until further Census data are available and comparisons can be made over time.

Income and Employment Structure

The level of income within an area is closely associated with its industrial structure – whether, that is, low-wage or high-wage industries predominate. Thus, average per capita income tends to vary inversely with the relative importance of agriculture within a state and also with the relative importance of resource-processing industries (those for which the products of agriculture and mining are important), since both these sectors are on the low-income-paying side. Incomes are positively associated with the relative importance of employment in the fabricating industries (whose material inputs are largely intermediate products), and these industries are important in the Manufacturing Belt states and in the Far West areas with the highest incomes.

Of course, there are substantial variations in income payments among the various industries within these broad categories, and variations tend to be reflected in the income levels of the states where they predominate. It is also worth noting that the level of state per capita income tends to be higher where there is a relatively large employment in the business services (industries at least one-third of whose output is purchased by other than final consumers); but there is no significant association between income and employment in consumer services. These findings should be particularly interesting to those who have been assuming that a shift of employment to *any* type of manufacturing and *any* type of services within a state is a sure path to high income levels.

More refined industrial-regional breakdowns show additional significant relationships. Among farmers, the only substantial regional variation in income levels is between the farmer in the South and the farmer in the rest of the nation. As a matter of fact, if price adjustments are made for commodities consumed by farm families, the 1949 *real* incomes of farm and nonfarm persons in New England, the Plains, and the Mountain regions were roughly comparable. In the Southeast, by contrast, the median income of white urban and rural nonfarm persons was about one and a half times as great as that of white rural farm persons.

It is clear that the average money wage in a state depends, in broadest terms, on the industrial and occupational composition of its labor force – that is, whether the major industries in the state provide low-paying or high-paying jobs. But wage levels, in turn, have an influence on the occupational and industrial structure of a state, so that these factors reinforce each other. In states where the average wage and salary earnings of workers are above the national average, workers tend to be concentrated in the higher paying occupations and industries. Moreover, in such states, the average earnings in *all* occupations and industries tend to be above the national average for that occupation or industry.[3] In other words, workers in relatively high-wage industries, like chemicals, as well as workers in low-wage industries, like apparel or personal services, will usually earn less for the same work in the poorer sections of the country than in the higher income states. Thus, income effects seem to be self-reinforcing in several ways: in terms of the types of industries attracted to a given state, the degree to which industries tend to be labor-intensive or capital-intensive, and the general wage levels set by local labor supply and demand conditions within a given labor market.

Differentials in Wage Levels

Among the many interrelated factors that determine differentials in wage levels and therefore in income generally, two are dominant: (1) the marginal productivity of labor (or the relative value of the product that a worker will turn out on the average within a given period), and (2) the relationship between labor supply and the job opportunities available within given areas. The latter is influenced on

[3]Frank Hanna, *State Income Differentials, 1919-1954* (Durham, N. C.: Duke University Press, 1959) Chapters 5 and 6.

the supply side by birth rates and migration, and on the job-opportunity side by the relative input-output access advantages for industry as discussed in earlier chapters.

The marginal productivity of labor has a distinct bearing on interstate differences in wage levels of workers in the same industry. In turn, marginal productivity differences appear to be related to differences in the proportion with which labor is combined with other factors, especially capital. This is true for both agriculture and manufacturing. In the study on which this shortened version draws, a detailed analysis was made of agricultural income data for 1950 and the period 1930-54, and of manufacturing income data for 1950 and the period 1919-54. The conclusions that were reached, summarized below, indicate the effects upon income differentials when these variables are considered.

Output per worker in agriculture, which varies greatly in the diferent states (in 1950 it ranged from $7,417 in Arizona to $1,089 in South Carolina), was found to be significantly associated with capital per worker (as measured by the value of land and buildings). Once variations in capital per worker are taken into account, no significant regional variation in output per worker can be detected, either at one point in time or, in terms of rates of change, over a period of years. This helps to pinpoint an important aspect of the low-income problem: It can be inferred that, while at present the output per worker in agriculture is, for example, very low in the Southeast, the introduction of more capital into its agriculture (assuming of course that it is sensibly applied) is likely greatly to improve output and income per worker in that region.

Interstate differences in labor income from manufacturing were also found to be highly associated with differences in the marginal productivity of labor and this in turn, as in agriculture, with the amount of capital that labor had to work with. Once the differences in the relative amounts of capital and labor used in production were held constant as among regions, results suggest that for most industries there is no significant regional variation in wages of production workers. But here it is important to note again that the differences in the amount of capital used within the same industry among the various regions is itself related to relative wage levels and that these in turn are related to the "pressure" of population numbers on wage levels – a point examined more closely in a later section.

Relative Rates of Growth in Per Capita Income

So far we have examined income differences at one point in time. What has been happening with regard to average income levels over time?

Rates of increase in per capita income levels among the states have varied substantially over the years for which we have income data, from 1880 to the present. As was noted in Chapter 1, over this period there has been a strong tendency for convergence in income levels among the regions and states. Whereas in 1880 regional per capita income averages ranged from a high of 211 per cent of the national average (in the Far West) to a low of 50 per cent (in the Southeast), by 1920 this range had narrowed to a high of 135 per cent and a low of 56 per cent, and by 1959 the income range extended from only 118 per cent at the top to 72 per cent for the lowest income region.

The trend towards equalization in income among the regions and states has not been constant, however. During the decade of the 1920's relative differences among the states in per capita income actually widened. In 1930, the Southeast's average income was at almost the same point in comparison with the national average as it was in 1880 (50.2 per cent compared with 49.9 per cent). Since then the forces of equalization have been dominant, particularly during the depression of the 1930's and during World War II. Since 1947 the rate of convergence has slowed down. Over the three-decade period from 1929 to 1959 the relative interstate variation in per capita income fell from 36 per cent to 21 per cent (see Table 22).

It should be noted, however, that although personal income per capita among the states has tended to converge since 1929, the *absolute* increases in total real income have not differed significantly. For example, between 1929 and 1959 per capita income increased in the Southeast on the average by $850 (in constant 1959 prices) as compared with an increase of $788 for the whole country. Thus, the progress towards equality in per capita income shown by the Southeast still has a long way to go because of its relatively low income at the beginning of the period. Also, the rank order of states in per capita personal income has remained virtually unchanged. Yet the progress made over the past three decades is encouraging.

Table 22. Per capita personal income, by region, selected states, 1959 dollars, 1929-1959

Region and state[a]	1929		1959		Increase 1929 to 1959		Ratio of 1959 to 1929	
New England	$1,718		$2,396		$678		1.395	
Maine		$1,178		$1,768		$590		1.501
Connecticut		2,018		2,817		799		1.396
Middle Atlantic	1,908		2,540		632		1.331	
Pennsylvania		1,520		2,222		702		1.462
New York		2,272		2,736		464		1.204
Great Lakes	1,574		2,337		763		1.485	
Indiana		1,200		2,102		902		1.752
Illinois		1,876		2,610		734		1.391
Southeast	714		1,564		850		2.190	
South Carolina		529		1,332		803		2.518
Florida		1,022		1,980		958		1.937
Plains	1,122		1,978		856		1.763	
North Dakota		735		1,526		791		2.076
Missouri		1,231		2,145		914		1.742
Southwest	908		1,828		920		2.013	
Louisiana		814		1,575		761		1.935
Arizona		1,159		1,959		800		1.690
Mountain	1,169		1,990		821		1.702	
Idaho		986		1,782		796		1.807
Wyoming		1,327		2,149		822		1.619
Far West	1,784		2,565		781		1.438	
Oregon		1,339		2,171		832		1.621
California		1,951		2,661		710		1.364
United States	$1,378		$2,166		$788		1.572	
Relative variation	35.8%		21.2%		—		—	

[a] Regional averages are total personal income for the region divided by population for the region, hence the weighted (by population) average of per capita personal income.

Changes in Employment Structure

What has been behind the convergence in income levels over recent decades? Our analysis would suggest that the most important single factor pulling the per capita income of the lowest income regions – the Southeast and Southwest – closer to the national average has been the decline in agricultural employment in these states (see Figure 21). The contribution of this factor is particularly striking in the Deep South – South Carolina, Georgia, Alabama, Mississippi, and Arkansas. Between 1920 and 1950 the movement of labor out of agriculture in these five states resulted in increases of from 24 per cent to 28 per cent of participation income per worker, as compared with a national average increase of 6.6 per cent attributable to this factor. In the Southwest (excluding Arizona where there was a below-average contribution) it resulted in increases of from 10 per cent to 19 per cent. The effect of the shift out of agriculture was important in the South because there the fall in the proportion of labor force in agriculture was relatively large and because differences in agricultural and nonagricultural income were extreme.

Figure 21
Increase in Participation Income Per Worker Due to Fall in Per Cent Labor Force Employed in Agriculture, 1920-1950

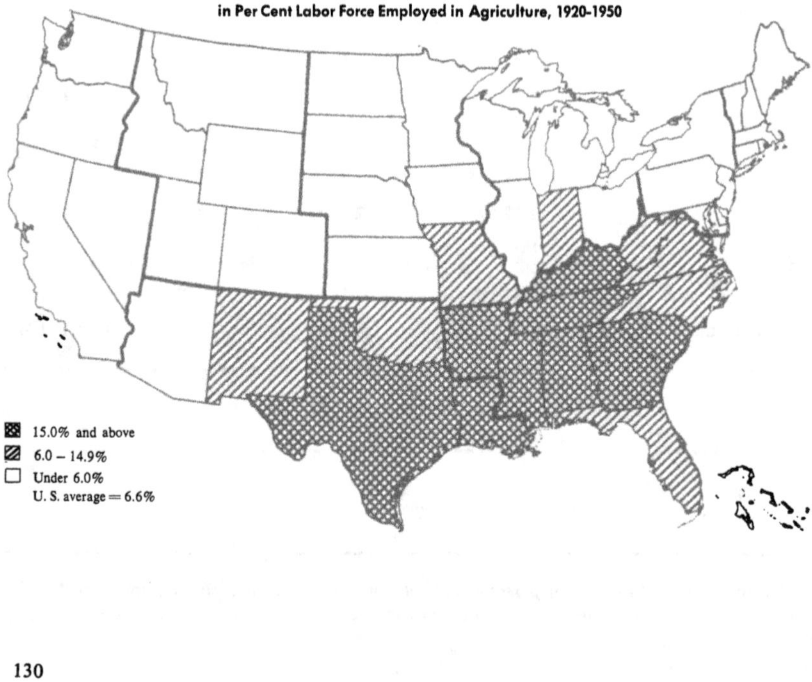

There has been an even stronger tendency for per capita incomes to increase in states where the proportion of the labor force employed in manufacturing increased very rapidly, and of course the greatest increases in income occurred in those states where the two tendencies, agricultural decrease and manufacturing increase, reinforced themselves.

There is a significant correlation between differential change in per capita income among the states and the changes in the relative importance of agriculture and manufacturing activities within each. Where the percentage of the labor force employed in agriculture tends to decline most and that in manufacturing to increase most, per capita income increases relatively the most. However, there is nothing inevitable about this relationship; rather it is a reflection of special economic and technical developments within each employment sector, and these can be different in different areas. When we get away from the national averages great differences can be noted in association between income and agriculture for the Northern and Western states as compared with that for the Southern states.

Changes in Capital-Labor Ratios

Changes in labor income in both agriculture and manufacturing have gone hand in hand with changes in the marginal productivity of labor and in the relative use of capital. Our analysis shows that over the 1920-50 period changes in agricultural output per worker (and therefore income per worker) were significantly related to changes in the value of land and buildings per worker. Except during the depressed thirties, changes in manufacturing wages were also found to be significantly associated with changes in the proportions of capital used. When capital was held constant, no significant regional effects were found in changes in income per manufacturing worker.

Income and Population

Changes in the marginal productivity of labor and in the relative use of capital are of course related to the labor market conditions. Per capita income is also related to the ratio of productive workers to total population within a given region. Thus, changes in levels of living are strongly influenced by changes in population. When job opportunities are expanding rapidly, population growth can go hand in glove with increases in per capita income, but when job opportunities are not expanding or are expanding only slowly, population increase may be a serious drag on wage levels and income. This is a highly complex subject and introduces so many unresolved questions that it can be dealt with here in only a generalized and speculative manner.

Conceivably, relatively low local wage levels and large number of unemployed or underemployed workers in a given area (say, a Southeastern state) might attract industry and capital investment in sufficient volume to bring the per capita income level up to the national average. However, industrial location has a logic of its own; for many industries, closeness to national or major regional markets or to input sources may carry more weight than lower wage levels. It is not a foregone conclusion, therefore, that inflow of capital and creation of new job opportunities will be fully adequate to absorb the natural increase in labor force and effect any significant improvement in living levels.

A sizable number of industries might well be attracted to the area over a certain period of time; yet the demand for labor which is generated might still be insufficient to absorb the labor force at wage rates comparable to the national average for the types of labor involved. Then not only would the "surplus" of labor persist, but the tendency toward low per capita income would be reinforced by the incentive of industries coming into the area to use more labor and less capital than in higher wage areas of the country. Under such circumstance, migration out of the area might well serve to raise average wages and per capita income.

One can conjecture that the amount of out-migration required to bring wages and income within a given area close to national averages would depend on many factors, among them: (1) the rate of natural increase in population, and of in-migration if any; (2) the ratio of labor force to population and the number of new entrants into the labor force; (3) the existing amount of unemployment and underemployment; (4) the extent of decline in demand for labor as a result of mechanization and related technological and organizational change; and (5) the rate at which new job opportunities are being created. All this can add up to the need for heavy out-migration from disadvantaged areas.

Birth rates in particular would influence the desirable amount of out-migration. For example, between 1940 and 1950, the rate of movement out of agriculture ran as high as 90 per cent in some Southeastern states (and of course geographic mobility was closely tied to this movement). For example, during the decade some 465,000 persons left agriculture in Alabama, amounting to a movement out of farming of 93.4 per cent. At the same time, Alabama's rural farm replacement rate was 203 per cent – that is, the number of young persons entering the agricultural labor force was more than double the number required to replace retiring farm workers and maintain the farm labor force at existing levels. (By comparison, New York State had a replacement rate of 115 per cent and California of 122 per cent.) Altogether, then, farm employment in Alabama was reduced by a total of a mere 127,000 persons – a decrease of 25 per cent.

Translated into geographic terms, a predominantly agricultural region may continue to be subject to underemployment and limited improvements in income levels in the face of substantial out-migration, as long as birth rates continue relatively high. Moreover, even if involving reductions in total numbers, out-migration cannot of itself be expected to increase levels of living. It would have to be accompanied by several changes – such as larger farms, a higher ratio of capital inputs, and a more efficient use of labor – which add up to a higher productivity per farm worker. Without these improvements the rate of increase in income levels can be painfully slow.

The experience of nonfarm depressed areas, such as certain of the coal mining areas of Pennsylvania, Kentucky, West Virginia, and Illinois, and the textile mill communities in New England, has been similar to that of the southern farm regions. Here, too, while large numbers of workers have left, many others have stayed on over the years in spite of unemployment or low-wage employment, and the replacement rates, in some instances, have continued to be very high.

One feature of the movement of persons within the continental United States seems to play a major role in the population-income relationship. When a region offers unusually attractive job (and living) opportunities, and when it can absorb new labor force from outside its borders at relatively high wages, it can and does draw persons from many parts of the nation and the cumulative in-migration can be large. Quite a different situation obtains in a region, which, in terms of relative job and income opportunities, is "over-populated." For this region the proportion of persons willing to leave the area to improve their economic situation becomes a critical factor. For the region that can absorb in-migrants, the characteristics of resident population are not significant; it can draw persons even from other high-income areas.

The foregoing suggests that migrants are likely to keep arriving into a region offering unusually attractive wages until the interregional wage differential is dampened, but that out-migration from any given area will not always be at the volume and rate called for by the objective situation (i.e., the wage and income differentials). In other words, under conditions existing in the continental United States, no one region can long be far ahead of all the others in its wage and income levels, but any one region *can* continue to have per capita income levels well below the national average.

Table 23. Net regional migration per 1,000 average population, 1900-1950

Region	1900-10	1910-20	1920-30	1930-40	1940-50
New England	91	48	4	— 6	— 1
Middle Atlantic	113	47	54	12	5
Great Lakes	33	72	55	— 4	13
Southeast	— 33	— 47	— 64	— 23	— 58
Plains	— 9	— 26	— 56	— 46	— 73
Southwest	176	41	27	— 39	— 10
Mountain	289	96	— 74	— 11	— 13
Far West	481	220	307	145	284

The figures on net regional migration (see Table 23) suggest that the migration movements have on the whole been into areas with expanding income earning opportunities and out of the areas with relatively limited job and income opportunities. Clearly it is not the *lack* of out-migration from the poorer areas, but the magnitude of out-migration required to achieve income equality (given the rate of population replacement in these areas) that is a basic difficulty facing the poorer regions of the country.

It is also clear that migration has been subject to major cyclical variations. Thus in the prosperous 1940's – a decade in which war activities stimulated movement – migration was two and one half times as great as it was in the preceding decade when job opportunities in the nonfarm sectors were scarce throughout the country as a result of the depression. These different reactions suggest that, with a continuation of the national prosperity, the magnitude of the low-income problem will continue to be reduced, if slowly. It is equally clear that if national or state policy would aim seriously at a more rapid rate of improvement in the income levels of the poorer areas, rather substantial programs serving to influence migration rates would be called for, as well as programs to increase employment opportunities where they are economically feasible.

Significant qualitative considerations should also be taken into account. The over-all effect of migration upon per capita income levels can be expected to vary with the characteristics of those who leave the area and of those who remain behind – whether they are in the labor force or not and whether they are older or younger persons, skilled or unskilled, white or non-white, and so on. The numbers-quality aspects are interrelated in a highly complicated fashion. One suspects that there are always both gains and losses income-wise and that the net result evolves in a highly dynamic fashion.

For example, the characteristics of the out-migrants will influence the over-all productivity level of the community, the nature of the local market (e.g., the demand for new homes and other new-family-oriented purchases), the costs of public services, such as education, and the ability of the community to finance them. What happens to the spirit of a community or region under the impact of out-migration is also no small matter. The qualitative aspects are elusive and hard to evaluate, but this is a subject deserving careful study when considering programs for raising income levels in areas which cannot adequately support their present populations. We must learn to deal with problems of "emptying out" in a realistic way, including consideration of help from national and state governments for "write-off" of public facilities and other aid to communities facing problems of declining population. Given the powerful forces at work, income levels in the poorer regions of the country will not be substantially raised in the next few decades unless imaginative and courageous measures are undertaken.

10. Approaches to Regional Development

Clearly, we are at an early stage of thought in evolving approaches to the development of our subnational areas. While essentially concerned with historical and formal analysis, the materials covered in the present study suggest the nature of the considerations that should underlie efforts toward area development or economic improvement.

Let us look at some general propositions about regional economic growth and area development.

1. Differential regional economic growth is an integral characteristic of our open, highly dynamic economy. As long as demand and supply conditions are subject to change, and regions have differing advantages and disadvantages for production, differences in regional growth must be seen as part of the total system, just as are economic specialization and division of labor. Periods of faster and slower growth over time may be expected for each region – both in volume of economic activities and in levels of living. Each growth period poses its own set of problems. This is as true when a period of slower growth follows one of rapid growth, as it is when a region has been in economic decline for some time. Similarly, an extremely rapid change in the employment structure of a given area may bring into being almost as many problems as a slowing down in growth.

Given our highly dynamic economy, *continuing* change is inevitable and therefore *continuing* adjustment is unavoidable. Problems of adjustment are always difficult and do not readily yield to solution. The forces at work are extremely complex and include physical, social, cultural, political, and psychological, as well as economic, factors, and the booby traps are numerous. It follows that activities inhibiting the needed adjustment of individuals, industries, or regions can be serious drags on the required adaptation. Subsidizing industries for continuance in uneconomic locations would fall into this category, as would efforts to delay the migration of workers from areas with little employment opportunity.

2. All the elements that are central to national economic growth are seen to play similar roles at the regional level. Included are the role of natural resources development, the key roles of manpower skills and human resources improvement, of aggressive entrepreneurship, of infra-structure (including transportation, water supply, power, etc.) and the associated external economies, as well as the ability to take advantage of new opportunities offered by new technological developments. (At the regional level, in addition, we find an increasing role played by amenity resources and the relative attractiveness of living conditions.) While we have come to take for granted the importance of these elements in national development — particularly with our current concern for aid to underdeveloped countries — their importance at the regional level is not fully grasped. Too often hucksterism, or the *selling* of the advantages of a given locality, is substituted for the more realistic concern for basic developmental forces. While there are very real limits to the developmental potential of any one region at any one period in time, judging by the more successful "area development" efforts, there is considerable play within these broad limits.

3. The study has underlined how important for growth of given regions is their capacity for attracting national industries — i.e., industries that produce goods for export to other regions of the country. Expansion of the export industries is at the core of regional economic growth. But substantial "internal" economic development is equally important. First, the direct and indirect impact on local income and employment of export industries covers a wide range from very great to relatively little; this is true of both the linked-industry effect (expansion of business services, the local manufacture of parts and equipment, etc.), and the effect on increased consumer expenditures. Second, "internal" factors have much to do with expansion of the local market and the extent to which this attracts industries producing for it. The kind of income distribution characteristic of a given region, for example, will affect the extent to which the local market develops.

In this context, growing market orientation and the tendency toward equalization of wages among regions are extremely important. The latter has been due to many factors, including over-all growth in national income, decentralization of industry, migration, unionization, minimum wage regulations, and the like. This is a slow and far from dramatic trend, but is firmly established. The narrowing of wage costs over time reduces their significance as a consideration in the location of economic activities and increases the significance of other factors. Over time, fewer and fewer industries are labor-oriented; market considerations, particularly, loom ever larger. This suggests that, where choices are possible, development policy should welcome new industries even though they push up wage levels.

4. "Growth" industries – those that are expanding in employment at a rate exceeding the average for all industries – favorably influence growth in the volume of economic activities within a region. But a region may grow by gathering in a greater and greater proportion of the slower growth industries. Also, industry aggregates include a variety of industrial subcategories, some of which are expanding more than others. Regions may experience growth even when they specialize in those industrial activities, such as agriculture or mining, which as a whole may be on the decline. As a matter of fact, regions can be somewhat like individual firms. Just as some farmers, or some coal mining firms or shoe manufacturing firms, tend to make extremely attractive profits and to increase their output in situations where competing firms are having serious trouble, so there are farming and mining and textile areas which, by intensive production and the growth of linked service activities, can experience growth when other areas with similar kinds of specialization are declining. Regions that are worried about a decline can learn some useful lessons from the flourishing firms in generally declining industries.

5. Also, while it is obvious that certain industries are more conducive to regional growth than others, not all regions have the relative advantages as to input-output access (i.e., relatively easy or cheap access to raw or semi-processed materials and to skilled and unskilled labor for their inputs, and to final or intermediate markets for their outputs) enabling them to attract such industries. Many can expect to grow only slowly on the basis of the industries for which they do have special advantages. Chapter 2 has stressed this point. In terms of such relative advantages as resources, markets, human skills, amenities, climate, and transportation facilities, some areas can hope to grow only by attracting labor-intensive industries; others by attracting certain processing industries which exploit relatively untapped natural resources; some may have advantages for certain

assembly operations; still others for relatively intensive recreation activities, etc. Attraction of industry is a competitive matter. A realistic appraisal of the region's relative advantages and disadvantages with regard to input-output access is an essential starting point for an understanding of its growth potential.

6. We have noted a spreading out of industry to the western and southeastern sections of the country, attracted by resource possibilities and even more by the newly evolving and rapidly growing regional markets. However, this decentralization is highly selective in geographic terms, involving essentially the growth of great regional production centers, often at the expense of surrounding rural areas and nearby small towns. The growth of large urban regions represented by such communities as Chicago, Minneapolis-St. Paul, Los Angeles, Atlanta, New Orleans-Baton Rouge, and Dallas-Ft. Worth, suggest this kind of development. The evolution of a complementary relationship between smaller production centers and large regional centers would seem in many cases to be a critical element in the growth of the smaller communities. In fact, what we seem to be observing is development within the western regions and the Southeast of "a hierarchy of cities," involving a large base of smaller communities, going up to the larger cities and state centers, on up to great regional centers – a phenomenon clearly associated with urban-industrial growth and one experienced much earlier in the northeastern part of the nation.

The clustering of economic activities into these great urban regions as well as into smaller urban centers has important implications for developmental efforts. The efficiency and attractiveness of urban communities become a significant ingredient in regional economic growth. City planning needs to be seen as a key weapon in area development.

7. We have seen that levels of living are closely tied to relative wage rates within regions, that these in turn are related to labor productivity, and that labor productivity is greatly influenced by the capital-labor ratios which characterize industries within each region, as well as by competency of management, labor skill, and effectiveness of industrial organization. A high capital-labor ratio is an important ingredient in providing a high level of wages within a region, but the relative use of capital as against the use of labor is itself related to wage level differences among the regions. Where wages are lower, more labor and less capital tend to be employed. Where pop-

ulation growth exceeds growth of employment opportunities, wages can be relatively depressed.

The fact that wages within certain regions have lagged behind those in others is not by itself enough to attract a large inflow of capital into the poorer regions. Flows of capital alone, therefore, need not bring about an equilibrium where wages for similar levels of skill are comparable throughout the nation. This suggests why additions to, and even existing members of, the labor force within a given region may not be fully employed and wage levels may be depressed. Under such circumstances, it is only through out-migration that upward pressure on wage levels can be exerted and per capita income raised.

As a general principle, it can be said that in a town or rural area where workers are paid substantially less than they could make elsewhere and where a basic change within five years or so is unlikely, a shift of some of the population out of the area might be just as important to the region's economic future as efforts to promote economic activities. Over-populated depressed areas tend to pull wage levels down all around and to be a drag on forward movement.

Every region in the country cannot hope to experience equally rapid increases in the volume of economic activities and in population. But every region *can* hope to enjoy a high and rising level of per capita income (as long as the nation's output and productivity increases), if it is willing to face up to the need for a degree of "emptying out" when the over-all situation with regard to relative advantages among regions calls for it.

In most such instances, significantly higher income levels can be achieved only by combining an effective economic development program with substantial out-migration. The experience of Puerto Rico is suggestive in this regard. It has taken a brilliantly conceived and executed economic development program, coupled with a rate of out-migration over the past decade high enough to keep the island's population at almost a stationary level, to permit the Puerto Rican people to realize a substantial continuous increase in the level of per capita income. Puerto Rico has not hesitated to help the migrants. Such a twofold effort is called for in a number of regions in the United States.

Encouragement of out-migration, under the appropriate circumstances, is dictated by two considerations. One is related to national economic progress. As far as the national economy is concerned, it is evident that the nation gains when the productive activities take place in those areas where net returns are highest. Anything that prevents an optimal locational pattern – such as continuing subsidy of industry in certain locations – can dampen national economic progress.

The other consideration is related to the welfare of individual families, for whom opportunities for jobs within the different parts of the country change over time. The ability of an individual to improve his lot by moving may have been most dramatic in the frontier-pioneering period, but it is a significant element in our type of system at all times.

One can infer from these two principles that a given regional growth pattern or type of development can be deemed "good" only when it contributes the most to over-all national advancement and also optimizes the employment and income-earning opportunities of individual families. Over time, with changing national demand-supply situations, this may mean a more or less rapid growth of population and economic activities within a given region. It follows that long-run national economic progress and long-run family welfare deserve a central place in any program looking toward regional development.

At the same time, however, the personal and social costs of migration cannot be overlooked in a democratic nation concerned with over-all welfare. It is unlikely, in fact, that an effective approach to migration can be implemented without consideration of ways to cope with these costs.

8. It is an essential ingredient of a sound program of economic development to encourage the location of new industries and work force in the most advantageous locations. In this, not only input and output factors over the foreseeable future must be weighed, but also the social and cultural opportunities likely to be offered to people at every stage of their life, but particularly when they are young. Many of our present depressed areas are by no means favorable environments for the growth of future citizens. Efforts to maintain economically and culturally poor areas of this kind are unlikely to produce *long-term* advantages, either for the nation or for more than a small proportion of the residents. Other localities that are in economic difficulties, however, possess useful social overhead facilities and good location, and have long provided an attractive social and cultural

environment. Having a substantial investment in such communities, the nation can well afford to take costly measures to protect its investment – if there are good possibilities of at least stabilizing the situation and preventing further decline. The protection of investment under appropriate circumstances is as sensible an objective for the nation as for the individual firm; but so is the write-off of investment when the situation calls for it.

9. The problems of subnational economic growth are so difficult and all-pervading that they must be recognized as the responsibility of all levels of government – from the local communities, through the states and multi-state regions, up to the Federal government—and of private groups at all these levels. While the local and state responsibility for economic development is increasingly being accepted, and while private groups have long taken a strong interest in the question of local economic growth, the Federal government's role has not yet adequately been defined.

The Federal government has taken an important step in recognizing national interest in subnational economic growth with the passage of the Area Redevelopment Act (1961), which is essentially addressed to the problems of depressed communities. While the focus on distressed areas may be quite appropriate from both humanitarian and political viewpoints, it should be recognized that from the economic standpoint (and also longer-run humanitarian considerations) the national interest and responsibility extend beyond the areas that already are in trouble. Efforts to *prevent* future distress and to cope with the problems of area adjustment to changing national conditions are at least equally important. The Federal government can help sound regional growth through strengthening information services, relating the development of natural resources (when carried out with Federal financing) to long-term regional economic requirements, providing flexible educational assistance to meet the different requirements of various regions, and through related efforts.

10. Given the complexity of regional economic development, it would seem particularly important to work out public policies that are realistic and selective – policies, that is, that relate effectively to the constantly changing national, regional, and local scenes. National and regional information programs, an awareness of regional needs, and encouragement of local planning are essential. Effective development programs require a firm foundation of detailed, up-to-

date knowledge and continuing research. It is necessary to know what is happening, to "take the pulse" of the regions, states, and metropolitan areas on a continuing basis. And it is necessary to plan the development activities with great care and sensitivity.[1]

High-caliber study and planning agencies within the various metropolitan communities and rural economic regions, as well as within the states and multi-state regions, are needed to probe continuously the problems and consequences of economic and other changes that are under way or projected, and to point the direction for sensible programs to cope with them. Not only area-wide problems and programs need attention, but groups with special economic problems, such as the non-whites, the young untrained persons, and the aged. Some states and communities have already started efforts along these lines but it is only a small beginning.

11. *Key element in developmental policy.* While specifics have to be worked out in every case, the broad requirements of developmental policy are suggested by the propositions discussed earlier, as well as practical experience. These can be summarized in terms of the needs for various kinds of investment: in human resources, in development of natural resources, in plant and equipment, and in social overhead.

(a) Investment is needed first in the human resources — to develop skillful, well-equipped individuals. This is a costly but key requirement for economic advance. An intensive effort to improve education, to prepare young persons for a lifetime of skilled, productive work, is the keystone of any development program.[2] Compared with other governmental measures that have been proposed, public investment in education promises the greatest relative returns. It might include Federal and state funds specifically provided for the low-income areas — with both total expenditure per pupil and the nonlocal share increasing in inverse ratio to the average level of income in the area. Such an effort might well focus on the establishment of quite large consolidated schools, bringing in students over a wide area, staffed by well-paid teachers, and providing far better

[1]See Committee on Regional Accounts, *Design of Regional Accounts,* edited by Werner Hochwald (Baltimore: The Johns Hopkins Press, 1961), and Charles M. Tiebout, *The Community Economic Base Study,* Supplementary Paper No. 16, Committee for Economic Development, New York (December 1962).

[2]The importance of education in this context has been stressed in two valuable CED reports, *Paying for Better Public Schools* and *Distressed Areas in a Growing Economy.*

than average general and vocational education. A highly developed system of vocational guidance should be attached to such consolidated schools. This would also be the best and most effective measure to help wipe out underemployment. Educated skilled persons can be counted on to seek out good employment and income opportunities and, equally important, situations favorable to continued development of the individual.[3]

(b) Investment is also needed in the development of natural resources. Here the Federal government's role can be significant, particularly if it were to seek to relate resource development in every region of the country to its special needs and possibilities. The states and regions have an equally large role. In some regions, the foundations for economic activities can be broadened and strengthened through the intensive development of under-utilized natural resources, such as forestry, water, and recreation (or "amenity") resources when such development promises – on the basis of realistic study – to attract new industries and service activities. Amenity resources can strengthen the economic base and are an appropriate subject for prudent investment.[4]

(c) Investment in plant and equipment and in infra-structure is the third leg of the development stool. In parts of the country that are characterized by very small, poorly equipped farms, incomes in farming can be raised in many cases by enlarging farms and by raising the productivity of farm labor through increased equipment (unless national policy were to dictate the taking of land out of agriculture in these areas). Encouragement of modernization of industry is another requirement, particularly in the older sections of the country. Techniques for encouraging such modernization have yet to be worked out but it deserves the best thought that can be given it. Investment in social overhead – in efficient and attractive cities, in transportation, and in other public facilities and utilities – is everywhere a basic need for sound economic growth.

Investment – in human resources, in natural resources, in capital facilities – this has always been the classic road to economic advance, and it still is.

[3] An important, if relatively small, start to advance training (and thereby assist the mobility of workers) has been made in the Manpower Development and Training Act of 1962.

[4] A noteworthy effort to strengthen resource development on a broad regional basis is being carried out by the Upper Midwest Research and Development Council. The studies and work of this group deserve the attention of all those interested in problems of regional economic growth.

SOURCES FOR TABLES AND FIGURES

Table

1. Adapted from U.S. Bureau of the Census, *U.S. Census of Population, 1950,* Vol. II, Part 1, Tables 6 and 15; and *1960 Census of Population, Advance Reports, Final Population Counts,* PC (A1)-2-52. The additions to total population for the Southeastern states and Texas for 1870 (see source note to Figure 1) have been allocated as urban or rural according to the weight of the urban population shown in the original census report. See also Tables P-4B and P-4C of E. S. Lee, A. R. Miller, C. P. Brainerd, and R. A. Easterlin, *Population Redistribution and Economic Growth, United States, 1870-1950* (Philadelphia: American Philosophical Society, 1957).
2. Unpublished data supplied by Richard Easterlin; C. F. Schwartz and R. E. Graham, Jr., *Personal Income by States since 1929,* U.S. Department of Commerce, Office of Business Economics, 1956; U.S. Department of Commerce, *Survey of Current Business,* August 1960, Table 2, p. 17. Deflators for 1880 and 1920 are 1929 GNP deflators used by Easterlin, transposed to 1959; 1940 is based on GNP implicit price deflator in *National Income and Output,* also transposed to 1959 base as given in *Survey of Current Business,* July 1960, Table 64.
3. U.S. Census volumes, 9th - 17th Census, as cited in statistical appendix to Perloff, Dunn, Lampard, and Muth, *Regions, Resources, and Economic Growth* (Baltimore: The Johns Hopkins Press, 1960), p. 615, A-6; *U.S. Census of Population, 1960,* PC(1)-C and PC(1)-D.
4. Lee, Miller, Brainerd, and Easterlin, *op. cit.,* Table M-8.
5. U.S. Census volumes, 9th-17th Census, as cited in statistical appendix to *Regions, Resources, and Economic Growth,* p. 615, A-7.
6. *Personal Income by States since 1929,* Tables 1, 2, and 3; *Survey of Current Business,* August 1959, Table 3; *Survey of Current Business,* August 1960, Tables 1 and 2, p. 17.
7. 1939: *Personal Income by States since 1929,* Table 1; 1958: *Survey of Current Business,* August 1959, Table 3, p. 15.
8. See sources, Table 13.
9. See sources, Table 13.
10. *Personal Income by States since 1929,* Table 3; U.S. Census volumes for 1954, as cited in statistical appendix to *Regions, Resources, and Economic Growth,* pp. 619, F-2, and 654-55.
11. See sources, Table 13.
12. See sources, Table 13.
13. Computed by Edgar S. Dunn, Jr., from sources as follows:
    Agricultural employment: 1939 — U.S. Census of Agriculture, 1940, Vol. III, Table 13; 1958 — U.S. Department of Agriculture, Agricultural Marketing Service, *Farm Labor,* LA 1 (1-60), estimates for state groupings adjusted.
    Mining employment: 1939 — *Census of Mineral Industries, 1939,* Vol. II, State Tables 2; 1958 — *1958 Census Mineral Industries, Preliminary General Statistics,* MIC(P)-2, May 1960.
    Construction employment: 1939 — U.S. Department of Labor, Bureau of Labor Statistics, *State Employment 1939-56* (1957), State Tables; 1958 — *Employment and Earnings,* Annual Supplement Issue, Vol. 6, No. 11 (May 1960), Table SB-5.
    Manufacturing employment: 1939 — *Census of Manufactures, 1939,* Vol. II, Part 1, General Summary, Table 6; 1958 — *1958 Census of Manufactures, General Statistics for States by Major Industry Groups,* MC(P)-5 (Preliminary), 1960.
    Transportation and public utilities: Same as construction employment.
    Wholesale trade employment: 1939 — *1948 Census of Business,* Vol. IV, Table 1 D, p. 1.09; 1958 — *1958 Census of Business,* preprint by state. Retail trade employment: 1939 — *1948 Census of Business,* Vol. I, Table 1 D, p. 1.06; 1958 — Same as wholesale trade employment.
    Finance, insurance, and real estate employment: Same as construction employment.
    Service and miscellaneous employment: Same as construction employment. Government employment: Same as construction employment.
    Total employment: A simple summation of the employment components identified in earlier sources.
14. See sources for mining employment, Table 13.
15. See sources for mining employment, Table 13.

16. Leland W. McCloud, *Comparative Costs of Competitive Fuels, A Study of Fuel Consumption by Manufacturing Industries in the United States, 1947,* West Virginia University, Business and Economic Studies, Vol. I, June 1951, Tables 4 and 5.
17. See sources for agricultural employment, Table 13.
18. *U.S. Census of Agriculture, 1940,* Vol. III, Table 8; and *U.S. Census of Agriculture, 1954,* Vol. II, Chapter IX.
19. 200 Sector BLS Inter-Industry Table — 1947.
20. 1939 — *Census of Manufactures, 1947,* Vol. III, State Tables No. 3; 1958 — estimated from *Census of Manufactures, 1958,* MC(P)-5, Preliminary.
21. Computed from *Survey of Current Business,* August 1960, pp. 17-22.
22. Computed from current dollar data in *Personal Income by States since 1929,* pp. 146-203; and from *Survey of Current Business,* August 1960, p. 17. Current dollar data deflated by implicit GNP deflator for the U.S.: 1929 — U.S. Department of Commerce, Office of Business Economics, *U.S. Income and Output,* Table VII-2, transposed to 1959, as given in *Survey of Current Business,* July 1960, Table 64.
23. Lee, Miller, Brainerd, and Easterlin, *op. cit.,* Table P-1.

Figure

1. Adapted from *U.S. Census of Population, 1950,* Vol. II, Part 1, Table 6, and *1960 Census of Population, Advance Reports, Final Population Counts,* PC (A1)-1. For 1870, adjustments were made for underenumeration of 1,260,078 (mostly rural Negroes) in thirteen southern states, by distributing the additional population among the twelve states of this study's Southeast region and Texas in the Southwest region according to each state's share of enumerated Southeastern-plus-Texas population.
2. *Regions, Resources, and Economic Growth,* p. 91.
3. Wheat and corn: *U.S. Census of Agriculture, 1950,* Vol. II, pp. 401, 403, 404, 410.
   Copper: U.S. Census, 1870, Vol. III, p. 767; *Mineral Resources, 1910,* Part I, pp. 170, 172 (Mine Returns); *Mineral Resources, 1930,* Part I, p. 706; *Minerals Yearbook, 1950,* p. 473.
   Coal: *Mineral Resources, 1921,* Part II, Back Folder; *Mineral Resources, 1931,* Part II, p. 430; *Minerals Yearbook, 1951,* p. 312.
   Pig Iron: U.S. Census, 1870, Vol. III, p. 603, American Iron and Steel Association, *Annual Statistical Reports, 1890,* p. 62, and 1910, p. 95; American Iron and Steel Institute, *Annual Statistical Reports, 1930,* p. 4, and *1950,* p. 18.
4. Unpublished series of data for state economic areas prepared by Donald J. Bogue and Calvin L. Beale.
5. See sources, Table 7.
6. 1939: *Personal Income by States since 1929,* Table 1; 1958: *Survey of Current Business,* August 1959, Table 1, p. 15.
7. See sources, Table 13.
8. See sources, Table 13.
9. See sources, Table 13.
10. See sources, Table 13.
11. National Coal Association, Department of Coal Economics.
12. See sources, Table 13.
13. See sources, Table 18.
14. See sources, Table 18.
15. See sources, Table 20.
16. See sources, Table 20.
17. See sources, Table 20.
18. See sources, Table 20.
19. See sources, Table 20.
20. *Survey of Current Business,* August 1960, Table 2.
21. *Regions, Resources, and Economic Growth,* p. 516, Table 171. Computed from unpublished data supplied by Richard Easterlin.

www.ingramcontent.com/pod-product-compliance
Lightning Source LLC
LaVergne TN
LVHW011805200926
848484LV00003B/786